Progressive Solution Prayers for Fruitfulness and Fulfillment

An Effective Approach to Solving Problems through Different Types of Divine Communications, Tested and Proven in Deliverance Ministration and Counseling

Dr. Pauline Walley-Daniels

iUniverse, Inc.
Bloomington

Progressive Solution Prayers for Fruitfulness and Fulfillment
An Effective Approach to Solving Problems through
Different Types of Divine Communications, Tested and
Proven in Deliverance Ministration and Counseling

iUniverse books may be ordered through booksellers or by contacting:

iUniverse
1663 Liberty Drive
Bloomington, IN 47403
www.iuniverse.com
1-800-Authors (1-800-288-4677)

ISBN: 978-1-4697-7344-5 (sc)
ISBN: 978-1-4697-7356-8 (hc)
ISBN: 978-1-4697-7357-5 (e)

Library of Congress Control Number: 2012903750

Printed in the United States of America

iUniverse rev. date: 4/18/2012

Contents

Acknowledgments ix

Foreword xi

Endorsement xiii

Testimony. xv

Part 1. The Progressive Cycle
   Introduction: Progressive Solution Prayers xix
   Chapter 1. Progressive Fruitfulness and Fulfillment. 1

Part 2. The Foundation of Divine Love
   Chapter 2. Foundational Solution Prayers 21
   Chapter 3. Prayer of Salvation: Falling in Love 33
   Chapter 4. Prayer of Repentance: Servicing Love
   Relationship 41
   Chapter 5. Prayer of Rededication: Reassuring Love
   Relationship 55

Part 3. The Progressive Love Life
   Chapter 6. Progressiveness: Growing Love 69
   Chapter 7. Progressive Prayer Life: Empowering Love. . .83
   Chapter 8. Progressive Bible Study Life: Equipping Love .93
   Chapter 9. Progressive Spiritual life: Active Love 105

Part 4. The Secular Endeavors

    Chapter 10. *Progressive Academic Endeavors*. 117

    Chapter 11. *Progressive Business Transactions* 129

    Chapter 12. *Progressive Employment*. 141

Part 5. The Relationship Cycle

    Chapter 13. *Progressive Relationships* 159

    Chapter 14. *Progressive Dating Relationships* 173

    Chapter 15. *Progressive Courtship Relationships* 185

    Chapter 16. *Progressive Marital Relationships* 199

Part 6. Realms of Fruitfulness

    Chapter 17. *Fruitfulness* 219

    Chapter 18. *Blessings* 237

Part 7. Realms of Warfare

    Chapter 19. *Uprooting Curses*. 251

    Chapter 20. *Breaking Yokes* 263

    Chapter 21. *Destroying Demonic Arrows* 273

    Chapter 22. *Spiritual Missiles*. 287

Part 8. Realms of Fulfillment

    Chapter 23. *Inheritance*. 303

    Chapter 24. *Fulfillment*. 315

    Reflection 329

Bibliography 337

Appendixes 339

    Decision 341

    Rededication 343

    *Pauline Walley Deliverance Bible Institute & Prophetic-
Deliverance Training and Theological Institute (School
of Intensive Training for Ministry and Leadership
Equipment)* 344

    Christian Books by Dr. Pauline Walley 347

    Subscription 352

ABOUT THE BOOK 353

ABOUT THE AUTHOR. 355

Acknowledgments

I am very grateful to the Lord God Almighty, Jehovah Jireh, the Great Provider, who has endowed me with such a unique ability to listen, hear, and understand the realms of effective prayers that transform life situations.

I am thankful to my editors, Kay Coulter, Rev. Ebere Trotman, Lilian Atter, Ruthy Kalu, Norma Clark Gaye, and Stella Kwofie, whose encouragement, suggestions, and assistance from the initial to final stages enabled me to complete this book.

Special thanks to my ministers and leaders at Overcomers' House Prophetic-Deliverance Church, Rev. Peace, Rev. Althia, Rev. Trotman, Evangelist Renna, and many others who have constantly used the materials from this book for teaching during fellowship meetings and proven the effectiveness of the prayers in this book.

My appreciation to my parents, Bishop Enoch and Felicia Walley, who taught me the importance of prayer; my husband, who has been supportive of my relationship with the Lord; and all the members of Pauline Walley Evangelistic Ministries, who have been there for me.

Finally, honor and respect to everyone who supported this book with their observations, experiences, and testimonies.

God bless all of you who tested and proved the effectiveness of *Progressive Solution Prayers*.

Foreword

Dr. Pauline has blessed the body of Christ with vital truths, teaching us how to pray more effectively. The disciples asked Jesus to teach them how to pray. Jesus gave them words to say and an outline to follow. It is scriptural to give people words to say in prayer so their prayers can be more effective and fruitful.

Jesus told us to pray to the Lord of the Harvest to send forth laborers into the harvest. There are different types of prayer and different purposes for praying. One of the major reasons for praying is that it gives God the legal right to override and supersede man's free will. God gave man a free will and will not destroy it, but He will temporarily supersede the free will, just like an airplane with the law of aerodynamics supersedes the law of gravity. It does not destroy the law of gravity, but overrides it with the law of aerodynamics. Prayer for people to change does not destroy people's free will, but it can override it. Prayer gives God the legal right to override His law of free will with the law of prayer. God will not make people go against His will, but He can make them willing to let go of it.

This book will enhance your prayer life. In fact, many readers will find their prayer life transformed. You will discover the power and purpose of praying much in your Holy Spirit–given language.

Nothing is done without prayer. After reading this book, much more will be accomplished in your life. Every Christian needs to read this book and put into practice its spiritual truths and practical principles.

Dr. Bill Hamon
Founder and bishop, Christian International Ministries and Christian International Family Church
Apostle and prophet of Christian International Apostolic Network
Author of ten major books, including *Prophets and Personal Prophecy* and *The Day of the Saints*

Endorsement

One of the most interesting statements I would like to make about my dear wife, Pauline Walley-Daniels, is that she has committed herself to writing one of the most powerful and wonderful books on prayer. I was amazed when I read the very first draft of the book, simply because it was profoundly inspiring and uplifting. The final draft of the book is truly a masterpiece for anyone who enjoys reading and praying and would like to gain a deeper understanding of the different types and purposes of prayers. For this reason, I am recommending this book of prayer as number one out of a million to both believers and nonbelievers alike.

Once again, this book of prayer is one of the most incredible books I have ever read. I have looked for a book like this one on many occasions, but so far, I have never spotted one on the market. I have read this one daily ever since the preliminary edition was published. However, this new edition is the latest and incorporates more sophisticated ways to approach several types of prayer. Brothers and sisters, please do not hesitate to purchase this prayer book; I am absolutely certain it will change your life for the better—in good and in bad times and in times of different needs or concerns.

Moreover, my wife is a prayer warrior to the world of prayer intercessors to whom she constantly communicates the power of prayer as one of the most important ways to develop a personal relationship with God. She very much loves to pray. I think she likes it more than she likes preaching or counseling; every minute of the day she sees a need for prayer. She prays constantly for our church members as well as for the sick, the poor, and the whole nation, and for people across the continents in different nations. On many occasions, I have insisted that she prays too much. However, she has been very grateful or thankful to me ever since she came into my life. I have acknowledged that I do not pray as much as my wife does, but I usually go into prayer when I feel there is a need for it, especially when I want to communicate and express my problems to God. She is a great motivator, inspirer, and encourager.

Finally, if we want our prayers to work, we must have faith and confidence and believe that God will answer our prayers. Matthew 6:9 stresses the immediate need for prayer. Here, Jesus Christ taught us how to pray because prayer is the foundation and one of the most fundamental ways to converse with the Holy Spirit on a personal basis.

Rev. Frederick R. Daniels
Vice president and pastor, Overcomers' House Prophetic-Deliverance Church
Bronx, New York

My Experience with Progressive Solution Prayers

In 2009 Dr. Pauline launched two prayer books, *Progressive Solution Prayers* and *Destiny Solution Prayers,* for preliminary assessments. As I read through *Progressive Solution Prayers,* I realized that it took me back to the basics of salvation. I was going through some personal issues and needed to experience God anew. In my struggles I found a prayer for my every need. Truly as I read these prayers and applied the words of the prayer to myself, I experienced a change with the movement of God in my life.

With this prayer book in your hands, your prayer meetings and fellowships don't have to be boring anymore. You don't have to search for words to communicate with your Father God; Dr. Pauline has found the words for you. Search the book and see where your needs are, and use it until your breakthrough comes.

Progressive Solution Prayers has a life all its own. I found that you must take this prayer book into your inner closet because it is so intimate. From the beginning you feel the anointing; it is life changing. It is for your own personal spiritual growth. I remember when I opened this book and started reading, I had to leave where I was and shut myself away in the privacy of my room so that I could bask in the movement of the Holy Spirit. It was glorious. The first time we used this book in our prayer meeting, just worshipping the names of God alone was awesome; the move of the Holy Spirit was so profound. This book has an experience for all who need to renew their intimacy with God.

Rev. Althia Rowe
Registrar, Pauline Walley Prophetic-Deliverance Training and Theological Institute (PWDI)
Bronx, New York

Part 1

The Progressive Cycle

Introduction

Progressive Solution Prayers

The prayers written in this book were birthed out of my personal encounters with the power of progressive solutions. The prayers have been used over and over again in healing and deliverance ministrations. The written prayers are not for recitation, but create a pattern that is meant to enhance your prayer life.

Many people cannot spend more than five minutes in prayer. While fasting, many people starve themselves around the clock, waiting for it to be over because they do not know how to pray and wail before the Lord. Although challenges drive many people into a fast, they do not know what words to use and what type of prayer to offer. This book has an abundance of solutions for you. Not only will you have enough words for your prayer, but your fasting time will be well occupied with spiritual works as you pursue and confront the enemy who has stolen something from you.

These prayers work. They will motivate you beyond reading to the level of experience and transformation. Your prayer life will be transformed. Your prayer language will improve. You will be well connected with the Holy Spirit and thereby have a deeper relationship with Him. Your Bible study life will become effective, because these prayers work and are based on scripture.

If your prayer need is not directly mentioned, you may fill in your needs with a pencil.

Note pages have been provided for you to monitor your own prayer life and results. For details on how to communicate your needs to God, refer to other books listed on the last pages, including my *Strategic Prayer Tactics I & II.*

Note Page

_____

_____

_____

_____

_____

_____

_____

_____

_____

_____

_____

_____

_____

_____

_____

_____

_____

_____

_____

Strategic Prayer for Progressive Solutions

Dear Lord and Father in heaven,
Hallowed be Your name.
I worship and honor You for my existence.
I praise and exalt Your name far above any other.
Lord, I ask that You would order my steps.
O Lord, guide and guard me into the realms of progression.
Please, Lord, grant me wisdom and knowledge for solutions.
Equip me with the kind of wisdom that would enable me
To devise solutions to the situations that confronts my life.
O Lord, you are the one who gave wisdom to Joseph to devise solutions
During the time of famine in Egypt;
You were the one who gave Joseph the wisdom to understand and interpret omens.
You were the one who set Joseph above all the problems that ever confronted him.
O Lord, You are the same yesterday, today, and forevermore.
Therefore, bless me with wisdom for solutions
And set me on the path of progression to excel in all my endeavors,
To be on top and never below,
And to be above and never beneath in Jesus' name. Amen!

Motivational Song of Victory

"Great God of Wonders"
Words: Samuel Davies, published posthumously in Hymns Adapted to Divine Worship, by Thomas Gibbons, 1769
Music: "Wonders (Sovereignty)," John Newton (1802–1886)

Great God of wonders! All Thy ways
are matchless, Godlike and divine;
But the fair glories of Thy grace
More Godlike and unrivaled shine,
More Godlike and unrivaled shine.

Crimes of such horror to forgive,
Such guilty, daring worms to spare;
This is Thy grand prerogative,
And none shall in the honor share,
And none shall in the honor share.

Angels and men, resign your claim
To pity, mercy, love and grace:
These glories crown Jehovah's Name
With an incomparable glaze
With an incomparable glaze.

In wonder lost, with trembling joy,
We take the pardon of our God:
Pardon for crimes of deepest dye,

A pardon bought with Jesus' blood,
A pardon bought with Jesus' blood.

O may this strange, this matchless grace,
This Godlike miracle of love,
Fill the whole earth with grateful praise,
And all th'angelic choirs above,
And all th'angelic choirs above.

Who is a pardoning God like Thee?
Or who has grace so rich and free?
Or who has grace so rich and free?

Prayer Observations and Experiences

Write down your observations and experiences as you say this prayer.

You may remember your dreams and some past occurrences while you are saying it. You may also receive a revelation. It is important that you make notes for future reference.

Observations

_____

_____

_____

_____

_____

Experiences

_____

_____

_____

_____

_____

Chapter One

Progressive Fruitfulness and Fulfillment

The work of the Holy Spirit is progressive. Every year, the Lord speaks to me about the need to walk, work, and live in the progressive realm of the spirit in fulfilling destiny. Walking and living in the realm of progressiveness takes one out of complacency and stagnancy. It takes a mature mind to understand the realm of progressiveness. The realm of progressiveness is a constant life of expectation and delivery. It is a realm in which one depends on the Holy Spirit for continuous instruction and direction. It is also a realm in which a person lives in steadfastness, whereby one is able to tolerate and overcome challenges and difficulties, knowing that the Lord is with him or her. A life without progression is a life that has no hope in destiny fulfillment.

Interruption with Progress: Destiny is an archeological excavation of the plans and purposes that God has for your life. Destiny is also an archeological discovery of your talent and ability that makes you to be productive and fruitful. Therefore, for you to be fruitful in your destiny you need to dwell in the realm of progressiveness, whereby your ability flourishes and yields productive results.

Although mankind was divinely blessed to be fruitful and to multiply from the beginning of creation, the enemy of progress has imposed an obnoxious role to impede humans' ability to fulfill destiny. Almost every facet of human existence has suffered from some form of satanic terrorism and demonic harassment. Hence many people have yet to discover their God-given blessings and unique abilities to be fruitful and fulfilled in their endeavors. Many have suffered unnecessary failures and stagnation without a taste of joy or satisfaction, because their destiny has been disrupted by destiny destroyers and destiny twisters. No matter what, the interference of destiny disrupters cannot stop the progressive work of the Holy Spirit.

The following testimony is my personal encounter with the progressive work of the Holy Spirit. This testimony reveals how the Lord has walked me through various stages in my life endeavor until this day. This testimony also forms the basis of the warfare and confrontation prayers that are seen throughout this book.

My Encounter with Progressiveness

Power of Progressive Prayer: I have had to deal with many difficulties and challenges from a very early age. I realized very early in life that I had to struggle for everything I did or tried to achieve. I had to pray fervently about everything I set out to do and continue to pray until I saw the manifestation of what I was praying for. The devil tried to frustrate every endeavor of mine by putting one obstacle after the other in my way. However, I was always able to overcome the enemy of my destiny and defeat his purposes with the power of prayer.

Divine Laughter: One major difficulty I had to overcome at a very early age was in the area of my health. The issue with my health started when I was a baby. Unlike other newborn babies, who come into this world crying as soon as they take their first breath, I came into the world laughing. My parents told me I laughed all the time and was a joy to anyone who came around me. Almost everyone who came into contact with me loved me and volunteered to babysit whenever my parents needed help. One such person was my parents' landlady, who lived next door to us.

Satanic Agenda: Madam Ruthie (not her actual name) was our landlady at the time and also a friend of my parents. Being an elderly woman and having had kids of her own, she volunteered to help my mother take care of me. She came to our house in the morning and bathed me while my mother took care of other household chores. Madam Ruthie was a big help to my mother, or so my mother thought. Unfortunately, Madam Ruthie had her own agenda. I believe the devil had a good idea of what my destiny was, and this landlady was assigned to twist it. She is an example of a modern-day Herod.

Matthew 2:3–16 says, When Herod the king had heard *these things,* he was troubled, and all Jerusalem with him. And when he had gathered all the chief priests and scribes of the people together, he demanded of them where Christ should be born. … And he sent them to Bethlehem, and said, Go and search diligently for the young child; and when ye have found *him,* bring me word again, *that I may come and worship him also.* … Then Herod, when he saw that he was mocked of the wise men, was exceeding wroth, and sent forth, and slew all the children that were in Bethlehem, and in all the coasts thereof, from two years old and under, according to the time which he had diligently enquired of the wise men. (Emphasis added.)

Just like the biblical King Herod who killed so many children in an attempt to destroy the destiny of baby Jesus, the Savior of mankind, Madam Ruthie tried to destroy my life and destiny. Her mission, as was later revealed to me, was to take away my joy and ultimately the smile and laughter that people loved so much.

Mysterious Ailment: Soon after I entered my teenage years, which was also around the time I became a very devout Christian, I began having severe headaches. Doctors failed to diagnose the cause of these headaches. I also had severe abdominal pains that came on at the same time I was having the terrible headaches. Doctors checked my stomach, including my womb, but nothing they found made any sense or explained why I was having the pains.

The Mystery of Midnight Prayer: I was in the living room praying one night around midnight. I was about eighteen years old and had just finished high school. The living room adjoined my bedroom. As I was praying, I heard a noise on the roof, as if somebody were walking up there. I wondered who it could be. I opened the bedroom door with the intention of going out to check when I realized that the roof over my bedroom had been blown off mysteriously. I immediately perceived that it was an act of witchcraft or divination. I know that should have scared me, but somehow, I wasn't scared. I went back to the living room and continued with my prayers.

The Enemy of My Destiny: Very early the following morning, Madam Ruthie came knocking on our front door. I went to open the door and her demeanor wasn't pleasant. Without even asking what had happened, she demanded to know when I was going to fix the roof of my bedroom. My first thought was: *How did she know the roof had been blown off, since it was not visible from where she lived or even from the front of the house?* My bedroom was at the back of the house, and the damage was visible only from there. I was so astonished but I was unable to ask her how she knew about the roof before she walked away. I discussed this with my Christian friends during our next fellowship meeting. We realized that the matter required warfare prayer, and we decided to uproot every satanic agenda that Madam Ruthie had planned against my destiny. We also agreed to hold constant and effectual prayer at our homes every night around midnight.

Midnight Prayer Exposed Spiritual Wickedness: As we started praying, the landlady became antagonistic toward me anytime she met me. One day, her hostility culminated in an altercation with me. It was then that she told me she had taken measures to make sure I would not amount to anything in life. Madam Ruthie also told me that the headaches I had been suffering were caused by what she had done to me during those times she had given me a bath when I was a baby. She wouldn't tell me exactly what she had done. According to her, all I needed to know was that she was responsible for it and was proud of it.

Divine Intervention: I took this matter to God in prayer, and He has faithfully come to my rescue. I have been healed of the headaches and the stomach pains, and I will forever praise Him for His goodness and mercies. All the challenges and difficulties concerning my health have been resolved, and I am now healthy enough to focus on fulfilling the calling of God on my life. My Christian life has been progressive ever since that time, and I look forward to doing as much as I can by the power of the Holy Spirit to advance the kingdom of God.

The Traits of Progressiveness

The trait of progressiveness is marked by symbols of pregnancy. The elements that represent natural pregnancy also reveal traits of destiny fulfillments. Until a cycle is completed, there will be no fulfillment, although there might be traces of achievement. Some problems come to us like the challenges of pregnancies, whereas other problems are resolved like going through the stages that culminate the trimester of a pregnancy. The following are instances of how the symbols of pregnancy affect the progressiveness of the universal world:

Two thousand nine was the year that marked the completion of a pregnancy cycle and the beginning of a new harvest. Like a pregnant woman, a month or year that carries the number nine (2009 / 2019) is a time when many people expected to complete the cycle of expectation. Waiting for nine months or nine years to deliver a baby, an idea, an ambition, or a dream has been a state of torment and harassment for some individuals. As much as the Lord is about to shake the United States in a manner that will affect many other nations, the Lord will still cause those in labor to enjoy His loving arms of protection at the point of delivery. Hence, years that are multiples of the number ten (2010 / 2020 / 2030) will be a time of abundance for those who have been in the labor room.

Two thousand ten was revealed to be a season of birthing of pregnancies in multiples. The process of birthing will cause some people to enjoy fruitfulness that will also cause them to be fulfilled, and those who have been in a state of barrenness and stagnancy will enter the realm of fertilization for multiple productions that will bring satisfaction.

Two thousand eleven is an extra measure for progressive achievements and new beginnings. The number eleven as an extra measure will enable people who have unique talents and abilities to get some form of help to step into the realm of their destiny. Those who are open hearted and have open arms would seek to assist those who have been lingering in stagnancy and rejection, irrespective of their abilities. Sharing brings harvest and abundance to everyone, including the needy and the underprivileged.

Fruitfulness: Fruitfulness is evidence of fertility, productivity, increase, abundance, and progressives. To be fruitful is to have the ability to produce. It is a state of fertility and prosperity. When people are fruitful, the work of their hands will yield abundance of profit. Whatever those people do would always prosper. Their relationships with others will be effective and successful.

Fulfillment: To be fulfilled is to be accomplished in one's performance. One is fulfilled when there is satisfaction in one's productivity and success. A relationship is able to bring a person to a state of satisfaction when the presence of one's spouse, friend[s], partner[s], or associate[s] produces joy and peace. One's business transaction is accomplished when there is fruitfulness and profitability.

The state of fruitfulness and fulfillment is a unique state of prosperity, where one enjoys the blessings of Genesis 1:28–30 and 9:1–3.
Genesis 1:28–30

> And God blessed them, and God said unto them, Be fruitful, and multiply, and replenish the earth, and subdue it: and have dominion over the fish of the sea, and over the fowl of the air, and over every living thing that moveth upon the earth.
>
> And God said, Behold, I have given you every herb bearing seed, which is upon the face of all the earth, and every tree, in which is the fruit of a tree yielding seed; to you it shall be for meat. And to every beast of the earth, and to every fowl of the air, and to every thing that creepeth upon the earth, wherein there is life, I have given every green herb for meat: and it was so.

Genesis 9:1–3

> And God blessed Noah and his sons, and said unto them, Be fruitful, and multiply, and replenish the earth. And the fear of you and the dread of you shall be upon every beast of the earth, and upon every fowl of the air, upon all that moveth upon the earth, and upon all the fishes of the sea; into your hand are they delivered. Every moving thing that liveth shall be meat for you; even as the green herb have I given you all things.

The Blessing: This 2012 is the year of fruitfulness in which the pregnancies that are matured and ripened will be harvested. Beloved, the years of your labor are ripe for harvest. Your harvest reveals your level of fruitfulness and maturity. If your pregnancies are overdue, then get yourself into the labor ward; you are due for delivery. This is the year when your fruitfulness will bring you to a place of fulfillment. The enemy shall no longer interfere with your rewards and benefits.

Your delivery could be a promotion to the next level. Your delivery could be restoration of that which has been stolen or taken from you. If your blessings have been twisted or switched, then expect to have them restored. If you have been cheated or replaced by another person because of unfavorable judgments, expect your restoration. If your relationship has been demoralized, expect restitution and transformation. Your loved ones will return home to you. Your restoration will bring you into fruitfulness and fulfillment. Where you have had struggles and challenges, you shall experience fulfillment. Wherever you have suffered lack and poverty, you shall enjoy fruitfulness and multiplication.

Deuteronomy 28:1–8, 11–14 says,

> And it shall come to pass, if thou shalt hearken diligently unto the voice of the Lord thy God, to observe and to do all his commandments which I command thee this day, that the Lord thy God will set thee on high above all nations of the earth: And all these blessings shall come on thee, and overtake thee, if thou shalt hearken unto the voice of the Lord thy God. Blessed shalt thou be in the city, and blessed shalt thou be in the field. *Blessed shall be the fruit of thy body, and the fruit of thy ground, and the fruit of thy cattle, the increase of thy kine, and the flocks of thy sheep* … Blessed shall be thy basket and thy store … *The Lord shall command the blessing upon thee in thy storehouses, and in all that thou settest thine hand unto; and he shall bless thee in the land which the Lord thy God giveth thee.* …
>
> *And the Lord shall make thee plenteous in goods, in the fruit of thy body, and in the fruit of thy cattle, and in the fruit of thy ground, in the land which the Lord sware unto thy fathers to give thee.* The Lord shall open unto thee his good treasure, the heaven to give the rain unto thy land in his season, and to *bless all the work of thine hand: and thou shalt lend unto many nations, and thou shalt not borrow.* … And the Lord shall make thee the

head, and not the tail; and thou shalt be above only, and thou shalt not be beneath; if that thou hearken unto the commandments of the Lord thy God, which I command thee this day, to observe and to do them: And thou shalt not go aside from any of the words which I command thee this day, to the right hand, or to the left, to go after other gods to serve them. (Emphasis added.)

Progressive Prayer Fast: Your blessings will be forcefully released through fasting and prayer. Sometimes, we need to break the gates of brass that surround a person in order to pull out the blessings the enemy has stolen. This can be done through deliverance ministration and warfare prayers, some of which have been inculcated into the strategic prayers presented in each chapter of this book.

Deliverance ministration is a spiritual surgery during which a demonic presence is removed from a person's life or environment to grant emancipation to the victim.

Warfare prayer engages the enemy in combat to defeat and overcome demonic terrorism and harassment.

Confrontational prayer means facing the devil in a warring fashion to demand the release of an individual who is being held hostage or in spiritual imprisonment. (See details of different types of prayers in my book *Strategic Prayer Tactics*.)

Therefore, to experience progressive solution, one has to apply a specific type of prayer as a remedy to a specific problem, so that one will be able to identify the result that was achieved from a particular procedure.

Note Page

Strategic Solution Prayer
for
Fruitfulness and Fulfillment

Problem
I need to maintain fruitfulness and fulfillment.

Situation
I am unable to reap the fruits of my efforts.
I am unable to achieve my projections.
I have yet to be fulfilled in life.
My life is a constant struggle for anything and everything.

Goals
I will be fruitful in all my endeavors.
I will achieve my goals.
I will be fulfilled in life.
I will not work for another to harvest my fruit.
No one will take advantage of me.
I will not live in poverty or penury.

The Authority of Scripture
Isaiah 62:8–9, Joel 2:19–26

Isaiah 62:8–9
The Lord hath sworn by his right hand, and by the arm of his
strength, Surely I will no more give thy corn to be meat for thine

enemies; and the sons of the stranger shall not drink thy wine, for the which thou hast laboured:
But *they that have gathered it shall eat it,* and praise the Lord; and *they that have brought it together shall drink it* in the courts of my holiness.

Joel 2:19–26
Yea, the Lord will answer and say unto his people, Behold, *I will send you corn, and wine, and oil, and ye shall be satisfied therewith:* and I will no more make you a reproach among the heathen:
But I will remove far off from you the northern army, and will drive him into a land barren and desolate, with his face toward the east sea, and his hinder part toward the utmost sea, and his stink shall come up, and his ill savour shall come up, because he hath done great things ...
And *ye shall eat in plenty, and be satisfied,* and praise the name of the Lord our God, that hath dealt wondrously with you: and my people shall never be ashamed. (Emphasis added.)

Prayer in Action
(Praise, Worship, and Adoration)
Lord, I thank You for bringing me through the past into this year.
Thank You for giving me this year as a season of fruitfulness and fulfillment.
Thank You for the promise of blessing upon my life,
That from today my labor will no longer be in vain—in Jesus' name.
I will not work for another to reap my harvest—in Jesus' name.
I will not toil for another to twist and switch my promotion—in Jesus' name.
I will not plant for another to steal my produce—in Jesus' name.
According to Isaiah 62:8,
"... the sons of the stranger shall not drink thy wine,
for which thou hast laboured."

Therefore my efforts shall not be in vain.
The enemy will not garnish my income and investment.
It is time for fruitfulness. It is a season of fulfillment.

Environmental Protection

In the name of Jesus and with the authority in the blood of Jesus,
I build a hedge of protection around my environment
Against any form of satanic army that shall rise up against me.
In the name of Jesus I raise a hedge of fire against any
Demonic host that stands against my prosperity
In the spiritual and the physical realms
And in the material and financial realms.
Let the blood of Jesus destroy any weapons of evil
That were ever sent against me
In the business and secular realm,
And in the academic and employment realms.
In the name of Jesus, I release brimstone fire to consume any
satanic locust
That hovers around my productivity and fruitfulness.
In the name of Jesus, I release brimstone fire against the demonic
cankerworm
That interferes with my prosperity.
In the name of Jesus, I plead the blood of redemption against the
Demonic caterpillar
That destroys the source of my efforts.
In the name of Jesus, I plead the blood of deliverance against
the evil of palmerworm
That crawls around my daily endeavors by day or night.
According to Joel 2:25,
"And I will restore to you the years that the locust hath eaten, the
cankerworm, and the caterpiller, and the palmerworm."
Therefore no army of destruction shall stand against me in Jesus' name.
No workers of iniquity shall enchant me in the name of Jesus.

Declaration of Solution

In the name of Jesus Christ, my Lord and my Savior,
I declare *[fill in the year]* as my year of progressive fruitfulness and
fulfillment.
In the name of Jesus, whatever I lay my hands on shall be fruitful.
In the name of Jesus, I shall be fruitful in my going out and my
coming in.

I declare that the Lord shall open unto me His good treasure.
In the name of Jesus, the heavens shall release showers of blessings
and rainfall unto me.
And the favor of God shall rest upon me.
I stand on the word of God in Joel 2:19 to declare,
"Behold, I will send you corn, and wine, and oil, and ye shall
be satisfied therewith: and I will no more make you a reproach
among the heathen."
Therefore, I shall no longer suffer poverty or reproach in my life.
In the name of Jesus, I shall not plant for another to reap my harvest.
Therefore, I shall reap the harvest of my field in Jesus' name.
In the name of Jesus I shall not work for another to gain my promotion.
Therefore, I shall be elevated to higher grounds in Jesus' name.
In Jesus' name, I pray and declare
That whatever I have spoken shall be accomplished.
Amen!

Motivational Song of Victory

"Praise to the Holiest in the Height"
Words: John H. Newman, "The Dream of Gerontius," 1865
Music: "Gerontius," John B. Dykes, in *Hymns Ancient and Modern*, 1868

Praise to the Holiest in the height,
and in the depth be praise;
in all his words most wonderful,
most sure in all his ways!

O loving wisdom of our God!
When all was sin and shame,
a second Adam to the fight
and to the rescue came.

O wisest love! that flesh and blood,
which did in Adam fail,
should strive afresh against the foe,
should strive, and should prevail;

and that the highest gift of grace
should flesh and blood refine:
God's presence and his very self,
and essence all-divine.

O generous love! that he who smote
in Man for man the foe,
the double agony in Man
for man should undergo.

And in the garden secretly,
and on the Cross on high,
should teach His brethren, and inspire
to suffer and to die.

Praise to the Holiest in the height,
and in the depth be praise;
in all his words most wonderful,
most sure in all his ways!

Prayer Observations and Experiences

Write down your observations and experiences as you say this prayer.

You may remember your dreams and some past occurrences while you are saying it. You may also receive a revelation. It is important that you make notes for future reference.

Observations

_____

_____

_____

_____

_____

Experiences

_____

_____

_____

_____

_____

Part 2

The Foundation of Divine Love

Chapter Two

Foundational Solution Prayers

Every good thing has a starting point. A relationship with the King of Glory also has a foundation. The beginning of a relationship with God usually starts with a kind of communicative process, which may come through reading godly material or offering a prayer or listening to a godly program. A foundational relationship with the Almighty God may also start with an encounter or response to an invitation.

Foundation of Divine Love
An invitation from God is a call into a love relationship. Responding to an invitation from God is like plunging oneself into a pool of fresh water. The love of God is a pool of living water that gives peace in the midst of a storm, joy like a fountain of fresh water, and celebration like an abundance of rain.

God is love.
Love is one of the major characteristics of His supernatural attribute. Thus, the Lord created mankind out of love. He breathed His own breath into mankind to give him life. He placed mankind in an environment of love, so that mankind could reflect His attributes toward nature and the supernatural work of His love.

- The air that we breathe oozes out of His tender love.
- The water that we drink springs out of the well of His love.
- Our surroundings are guarded with the plantation of His love.
- Our garden is decorated with flowers of love that produce aromatic fragrance for affection.

Agape Love: The love of God is referred to as agape. It is a perfect love that connects the creator with His creatures. It is an unconditional love without blemish. It is the kind of love that does not retain evil.

- Agape love is the kind that tolerates another's misbehavior in the face of judgment.
- Agape love is the instrument that endures another's weakness in the midst of pain.
- Agape love is the kind of love that knows no envy or jealousy.
- Agape love is the kind of love that does not cohabit with strife or malice.
- Agape love is the love that is sincere without deception.
- Agape love is the love that is honest and faithful.
- Agape love is the love that has no room for accusation or fault finding.
- Agape love is the love that respects and honors.
- Agape love is the love that corrects and restores.
- Agape love is the love that forgives and forgets.
- Agape love is the love that seeks another's progress and promotion.
- Agape love is the love that encourages achievements and fulfillments.
- Agape love is the love that fosters fertility and productivity.
- Agape love is the love that enhances fruitfulness and abundance.
- Agape love is the love that does not destroy the reproductive seed of destiny.

- Agape love does not hunt another's power of achievements.
- Agape love seeks understanding in times of incidents and accidents.

Philia: *Philia* means "friendship." It is also known as brotherly or sisterly love. Where there is agape, philia is naturally produced. Philia is the natural love that exists between two people irrespective of their biological relationship or family ties. Philia is the type of love that produces loyalty, commitment, dedication, and familiarity among people from different biological backgrounds and of different descents. Philia is also the type of love that holds both lovers and family members together. Wherever philia is rooted in agape love, family members, neighbors, and strangers can dwell together in peace and with understanding.

Eros: Eros is from a Greek word, *erotas,* which means "romantic love." It is a passionate love that desires sensual affection and leads to dating, courtship, and then marriage. More often than not, Eros is connected to a sexual relationship. However, Eros is effective if it springs out of agape and also has a connection to philia. Thus, Eros stands a better chance of growing like a tree planted by rivers of living waters, because the parties involved are lifetime friends whose relationship is embedded in the perfect love of God.

Storge: Storge is the type of love that exists between parents and their children. It is a natural affection that springs out of biological offspring because of blood ties or genetic affection. Parental love is deeply rooted in agape.

My First Encounter with Divine Love
When the evil plot staged by Madam Ruthie began to take effect in my life at an early age, my parents unconsciously treated me as though I were an element of shame and disgrace to their progress. For instance, my mother was very impatient with me. She scolded and punished me for everything I did right or wrong. I felt hated by my parents, whereas everyone around me liked me for my constant smile and laughter.

In view of the dislike from my parents, I started to search for the love of God at a very tender age. At age eight, I encountered the love of Jesus Christ in an open vision while I was seated in my primary school classroom. Although I did not know what revelation was at the time, I felt a deep protection in the arms of the Lord. Fortunately, my parents kept us in close contact with Bible studies and prayer fellowship every morning when we woke up and at night before we went to bed. Also, I had a private tutor who was a Christian, so I narrated my visions and all my experiences to him, and he used the Bible to interpret the childhood revelations that I received.

Various forms of foundational activities connect a person to God from the start. There are also some other activities that reconnect those who have wandered far away from God the Father.

A connection with the Lord is like a love affair, where a lady suddenly finds her love in the type of man she has been dreaming of. Get ready for a passionate love relationship with your Maker as you learn how to approach Him just as you are.

The next two chapters offer various types of prayers that will plug you into the heart of God for a fatherly relationship if you want to feel a parental touch from the Creator of humanity. These prayers will also connect you to God for a spiritual relationship if that is your desire.

Just like every human relationship has a beginning that forms the root of existence, there is always an experience that connects humanity to God, our Creator.

Although human beings are created in God's image according to His likeness, sin separated us from God. In view of our human errors and weaknesses, we have wandered far away from the love of God, so we need a turning point to return to Him. For us to gain access to His presence, we need a kind of spiritual communication such as this:

- Prayer of Salvation as the beginning of falling in love
- Prayer of Repentance as a point of restoring love
- Prayer of Rededication as a form of reassuring love
- Prayer of Confession as a form of releasing hurt
- Prayer of Forgiveness as a form of separating love from offense

Some of these prayers, which have been provided in the subsequent chapters, will guide you to plug in and will reconnect you to the presence of God.

Luke 15:3–10 says,

> And he spake this parable unto them, saying,
> What man of you, having an hundred sheep, if he lose one of them, doth not leave the ninety and nine in the wilderness, and go after that which is lost, until he find it?
> And when he hath found it, he layeth it on his shoulders, rejoicing.
> And when he cometh home, he calleth together his friends and neighbours, saying unto them, Rejoice with me; for I have found my sheep which was lost.
> I say unto you, that likewise joy shall be in heaven over one sinner that repenteth, more than over ninety and nine just persons, which need no repentance.
> Either what woman having ten pieces of silver, if she lose one piece, doth not light a candle, and sweep the house, and seek diligently till she find it?
> And when she hath found it, she calleth her friends and her neighbours together, saying, Rejoice with me; for I have found the piece which I had lost.
> Likewise, I say unto you, there is joy in the presence of the angels of God over one sinner that repenteth.

Note Page

_____

_____

_____

_____

_____

_____

_____

_____

_____

_____

_____

_____

_____

_____

_____

_____

Strategic Solution Prayer
for
Foundational Connection to the Creator

The Problem
I need a foundational connection to the Creator.
I need to be plugged into God as my Creator.

The Situation
I don't know what it means to be plugged into God.
I need to know God as my Creator and Father.
I want to stay connected to the Almighty God.

The Goal
I will be connected to God my Creator and stay connected forever.

The Authority of Scripture
Luke 15:8
Either what woman having ten pieces of silver, if she lose one
piece, doth not light a candle, and sweep the house, and seek
diligently till she find it?

Prayer in Action
(Praise, Worship, and Adoration)
O dear Lord, my God,
It's exciting to know that
My Creator is interested in me
And that He will be glad to have me plugged into Him

So I can be connected to His heart.
Lord, I am thrilled to discover this unique opportunity.
O Lord, let this foundational prayer bring me
An exciting encounter that will never fade away,
That I may know You, Almighty God, for myself,
And I may love You with all my heart.
O Lord, bless me that I may be blessed.
O Lord, hold me that I may be protected in Your arms.
Lead me through this foundational relationship,
That I may discover You beyond imagination.
O Lord, reveal Your love to me,
That I may experience You in reality.
Thank you, Lord, for being my Creator.
Thank you for bringing me to a new beginning in my destiny.
Hallelujah! Amen!

Motivational Song of Victory

"Lord, I'm Coming Home"
Music: William J. Kirkpatrick, published 1892
Scripture: Luke 15:18

I've wandered far away from God,
Now I'm coming home;
The paths of sin too long I've trod,
Lord, I'm coming home.

Refrain
Coming home, coming home,
Nevermore to roam;
Open wide Thine arms of love,
Lord, I'm coming home.

I've wasted many precious years,
Now I'm coming home;
I now repent with bitter tears,
Lord, I'm coming home.

I'm tired of sin and straying, Lord,
Now I'm coming home;
I'll trust Thy love, believe Thy word,
Lord, I'm coming home.

My soul is sick, my heart is sore,
Now I'm coming home;
My strength renew, my home restore,
Lord, I'm coming home.

My only hope, my only plea,
Now I'm coming home;
That Jesus died, and died for me,
Lord, I'm coming home.

I need His cleansing blood, I know,
Now I'm coming home;
O, wash me whiter than the snow,
Lord, I'm coming home.

Prayer Observations and Experiences

Write down your observations and experiences as you say this prayer.

You may remember your dreams and some past occurrences while you are saying it. You may also receive a revelation. It is important that you make notes for future reference.

Observations

_____

_____

_____

_____

_____

Experiences

_____

_____

_____

_____

_____

Chapter Three

Prayer of Salvation: Falling in Love

The Prayer of Salvation is one of the major foundational steps you need to access the presence of God. It is the key, and the password or code you need to open the door that leads into His presence.

Salvation
Salvation means falling in love with the Lord. It is a state of having a passionate desire to give your life to Him. It is a process of sowing your life into Christ Jesus, so that He will cover you like soil covers a seed that falls onto fertile ground.

When you are covered in the ground that represents the love of Christ Jesus, you will die to yourself, and the Lord will come alive in you.

Thus you will be saturated with the love of God and begin to reflect the love of Jesus Christ, who died to save your soul from sin and redeemed you from the realm of condemnation.

Prayer of Salvation: The Prayer of Salvation is the initial stage of falling in love with the Lord. You have been yearning and dreaming of a kind of love life that is full of passion and affection. Your dream is to connect with a person who will understand your needs and be a solution-oriented life partner who will seek the best avenue to satisfy your soul.

This prayer will help you discover Christ Jesus as the One who has already loved you with passion, and has already made provision for the comfort of your soul.

Also, for you to enjoy this prayer, you need to have a personal relationship with Jesus Christ as your Lord and Savior. If you have no relationship with Him, you will not have access to His presence. The following prayer of salvation will lead you to invite Jesus into your heart, so that you can experience His love in your life. You will then enjoy the sweet fellowship of having Him as your Lord and Savior.

Note Page

Strategic Solution Prayer
to
Fall in Love with God the Father

The Problem
I need to *fall in love with God* as my Father.

The Situation
I don't know what it means *to love the Lord.*
I don't know what it means to have a *relationship with God.*
I need to know Jesus Christ as my Lord and Savior.
I want to be secured in the arms of the Lord as the lover of my soul.

The Goals
I will have a father-child relationship with the Lord.
I will experience the secured arms of love in Christ Jesus.

The Authority of Scripture
John 1:12 and 16–17; Acts 16:30–31

John 1:12
But as many as received him, to them gave he power to become
the sons of God, even to them that believe on his name:

John 3:16–17
For God so loved the world, that he gave his only begotten
Son, that whosoever believeth in him should not perish, but

have everlasting life. For God sent not his Son into the world to condemn the world; but that the world through him might be saved.

Acts 16:30–31
And brought them out, and said, Sirs, what must I do to be saved? And they said, Believe on the Lord Jesus Christ, and thou shalt be saved, and thy house.

Prayer in Action
(Praise, Worship, and Adoration)

Father God, thank you for creating me.
Thank you for giving me the privilege of life.
Thank you for giving me the opportunity to desire a relationship with You.
Lord, I need You to be my Father and Redeemer.
You died on the cross to set me free from sin.
You shed Your blood to wash away my sin.
Therefore I invite You into my life today.
O Lord Jesus Christ,
Come into my heart today.
Forgive me of my sins and wash me in the blood
That You shed on the cross of Calvary.
Dear Lord, take over my whole life and being.
Hold me like a newborn baby in your arms.
Teach me to speak and walk all over again.
Fill me with Your Holy Spirit,
That I may live according to Your precepts and Your will.
Guard and lead me.
Instruct and direct my life and ways
That I will be Yours and Yours alone.
Let me experience Your love
That I may be secured in Your arms of love.
Thank You, Lord, for accepting me into Your presence.
Thank You for agreeing to be the lover of my soul.
Thank You for agreeing to be my Lord and Savior.
In Jesus' name I pray.
Amen!

Motivational Song of Victory

"Just As I Am"
Words: Charlotte Elliott, 1835
Music: "Woodworth," William B. Bradbury, *Mendelssohn Collection,*
or *Third Book of Psalmody* (New York: 1849)

> Just as I am, without one plea,
> But that Thy blood was shed for me,
> And that Thou bidst me come to Thee,
> O Lamb of God, I come, I come.
>
> Just as I am, and waiting not
> To rid my soul of one dark blot,
> To Thee whose blood can cleanse each spot,
> O Lamb of God, I come, I come.
>
> Just as I am, though tossed about
> With many a conflict, many a doubt,
> Fightings and fears within, without,
> O Lamb of God, I come, I come.
>
> Just as I am, poor, wretched, blind;
> Sight, riches, healing of the mind,
> Yea, all I need in Thee to find,
> O Lamb of God, I come, I come.

Just as I am, Thou wilt receive,
Wilt welcome, pardon, cleanse, relieve;
Because Thy promise I believe,
O Lamb of God, I come, I come.

Just as I am, Thy love unknown
Hath broken every barrier down;
Now, to be Thine, yea, Thine alone,
O Lamb of God, I come, I come.

Just as I am, of that free love
The breadth, length, depth, and height to prove,
Here for a season, then above,
O Lamb of God, I come, I come!

Prayer Observations and Experiences

Write down your observations and experiences as you say this prayer.

You may remember your dreams and some past occurrences while you are saying it. You may also receive a revelation. It is important that you make notes for future reference.

Observations

_____

_____

_____

_____

_____

Experiences

_____

_____

_____

_____

_____

Chapter Four

Prayer of Repentance: Servicing Love Relationship

Repentance

Repentance is a process of building healthy bridges in the environment of love. It is a state of clearing the old rugged life of pain, hurt, and disappointment in order to restore and create an environment of love.

Repentance is a process of washing, cleaning, and cleansing one's heart from dusty and rusty impediments that hinder one from receiving and sharing pure love from a healthy heart.

The Process of Repentance

The process of repentance revolves around forgiveness, whereby you forgive those who have offended you while you also seek forgiveness from those whom you have offended consciously or unconsciously. Without forgiveness, repentance is not effective. The act of repentance brings a person to a place of surrender and releasing oneself from a type of imprisonment. Anytime you hold someone in unforgiveness, your relationship with the Lord is severed. Your prayer life suffers delay and denial. Unforgiveness creates impediments in your relationship pipeline. Therefore, in order to receive forgiveness, you need to repent for allowing unforgiveness in your heart. Your heart is supposed to be the temple of the living God. Therefore, your heart must be kept pure and far away from impediments that will cause hindrances in your life and environment.

The following testimony illustrates an experience that one of my protégés encountered in the realms of forgiveness. Her name has been changed to Sally to protect her privacy.

Sally's Encounter with Forgiveness

Sally: I did not even know that I was still harboring ill feelings toward this man who broke my heart. As Dr. Pauline began to pray with me, the moment she began to pray for him, tears began to run down my face and I felt a release in my heart. I was already on a fast that day, so Dr. Pauline instructed me to go and pray and allow God to heal me completely.

This man had sought my forgiveness for what he did to me, but I was still very hurt and not letting go of the issue because I felt he still owed me an explanation. Dr. Pauline counseled me and said, "You will know you have really forgiven someone when you no longer demand an explanation or bring up the issue that caused the feelings of retaliation and resentment." Dr. Pauline advised me that since this man has sought my forgiveness, I have to offer forgiveness to him. I prayed over it for a couple of days in order to allow God to wipe the hurt away. I mustered the strength to call the man and told him that I have forgiven him. I was no longer interested in an explanation but wanted to let him know that I forgive him.

Thereafter, I was able to make peace with my cousins who I had been separated from for a couple of years due to some family contentions that happened. I took the first step in breaking the silence between my cousins and me.

After I did all those things, I realized that I could hear from God much better and more clearly. For over a year I had realized that my relationship with God was different. I was not feeling Him as close as I used to. I was fasting and praying and going to all the church services, but I realized that I did not have that moment-by-moment leading of the Holy Spirit that I used to enjoy.

Do you want to experience an intimate relationship with the Holy Spirit? Get rid of unforgiveness. It is no accident that in John 20:19–23 when the disciples receive the Holy Spirit as Jesus breathes on them, He immediately follows with a statement about forgiveness. "And when He had said this, He breathed on them, and said to them, 'Receive the Holy Spirit. If you forgive the sins of any, they are forgiven them; if you retain the sins of any, they are retained'" (John 20:22–23). Jesus makes it clear that we have the power to forgive through the Holy Spirit. The Bible also says that he who knows to do well and does not do it is sinning. So if you know you should forgive someone and you don't do it, it is a sin against God. The more you stay in unforgiveness, the more sin you attract and the harder it is for God to hear and answer your prayers. This is the reason Jesus said, "For if you forgive men their trespasses, our heavenly Father will also forgive you. But if you do not forgive men their trespasses, neither will your Father forgive your trespasses" (Matthew 6:14–15).

Now the most important relationship in my life has been restored and my heart and mind are at peace. I am now more conscious of the way I see people, the way I perceive people and making sure that I am not holding anyone in my heart. Also when someone makes me angry I try to let it go as quickly as possible, because when I am angry, I cannot hear from God.

And thanks to Dr. Pauline, I now have a greater understanding of forgiveness. The act of "forgive and forget" is truly possible. I hear people say, "I will forgive but I will never forget." Just like forgiveness is a choice, so is forgetting. We can choose to forget or choose to brood over the issue. Sometimes we brood over issues subconsciously, but it all contributes to and strengthens the power of unforgiveness. Like love, the more you think about the one you love, the more deeply you fall in love with them. Likewise the more you think about the fault someone did to you, the deeper you fall into the realm of unforgiveness. The saying that "time heals all wounds" is true, because over time you tend to forget, and as you forget, it makes it easier to forgive.

That's all I have for now, Dr. Pauline. Maybe I will have Part Two later :). Thanks for urging me to write it. I have learned even more, and I understand even better than I thought.

I love you … Happy Mother's Day in advance. You have really been a mother to me and I love you so much!

Prayer of Repentance

The Prayer of Repentance is a major step in the foundational process that opens up communication with the Lord. Repentance is one of the strongest access codes to the heart of God. Without repentance, your prayer will be like a bouncing ball over your head. The more you pray, the more it seems as though your prayer hits the roof over your head and bounces back to you.

Then you will feel like screaming, "Where are you, Lord? Why is my prayer not going anywhere? Aren't you my Creator?"

Well, there is a blockage somewhere, so your prayer is not flowing through. You need to clean up the drainage. It's time for repentance. It's not a choice—it's a requirement. You need to repent.

The prayer of repentance is important if you are struggling with a sinful character and behavior. Sin blocks you from the presence of God, and your prayers bounce back to you like a basketball. You must cleanse yourself with this prayer in order to gain access to the presence of the Lord, to enjoy love.

Note Page

_____

_____

_____

_____

_____

_____

_____

_____

_____

_____

_____

_____

_____

_____

_____

_____

_____

_____

_____

_____

Strategic Solution Prayer
for
Deliverance from Enticement to Sin

The Problem

I am surrounded by the temptation to sin.

The Situation

It seems as though I am not able to get away from sin.
My behavior seems to be offensive to people.
People are always offended by what I say or do.
Any attempt I make to stay away from sin seems impossible.

The Goals

I will be able to stay away from sin.
I will stop creating offenses that hurt people's feelings.
I will be able to apologize and move on without falling into the
same situation again.

The Authority of Scripture
Psalm 51:1–7, Zechariah 4:6, 1 John 1:9-10

Psalm 51:1–7
To the chief Musician, a Psalm of David, when Nathan the
prophet came unto him, after he had gone in to Bathsheba.
Have mercy upon me, O God, according to thy loving kindness:
according unto the multitude of thy tender mercies blot out my
transgressions. Wash me thoroughly from mine iniquity, and

cleanse me from my sin. For I acknowledge my transgressions: and my sin is ever before me. Against thee, thee only, have I sinned, and done this evil in thy sight: that thou mightest be justified when thou speakest, and be clear when thou judgest. Behold, I was shapen in iniquity; and in sin did my mother conceive me. Behold, thou desirest truth in the inward parts: and in the hidden part thou shalt make me to know wisdom.

Purge me with hyssop, and I shall be clean: wash me, and I shall be whiter than snow. Make me to hear joy and gladness; that the bones which thou hast broken may rejoice. Hide thy face from my sins, and blot out all mine iniquities Create in me a clean heart, O God; and renew a right spirit within me. Cast me not away from thy presence; and take not thy holy spirit from me. Restore unto me the joy of thy salvation; and uphold me with thy free spirit. Then will I teach transgressors thy ways; and sinners shall be converted unto thee.

Deliver me from blood guiltiness, O God, thou God of my salvation: and my tongue shall sing aloud of thy righteousness. O Lord, open thou my lips; and my mouth shall shew forth thy praise. For thou desirest not sacrifice; else would I give it: thou delightest not in burnt offering. The sacrifices of God are a broken spirit: a broken and a contrite heart, O God, thou wilt not despise.

Do good in thy good pleasure unto Zion: build thou the walls of Jerusalem. Then shalt thou be pleased with the sacrifices of righteousness, with burnt offering and whole burnt offering: then shall they offer bullocks upon thine altar.

Zechariah 4:6

Then he answered and spake unto me, saying, This is the word of the Lord unto Zerubbabel, saying, Not by might, nor by power, but by my spirit, saith the Lord of hosts.

I John 1:9-10

If we confess our sins, he is faithful and just to forgive us *our* sins, and to cleanse us from all unrighteousness.
If we say that we have not sinned, we make him a liar, and his word is not in us.

Prayer in Action
(Praise, Worship, and Adoration)
Dear Lord Jesus Christ,
I come before You to repent of my sin.
Lord, I need You to help me so I will no longer be an offense to anyone.
For I cannot help myself except You help me.
Lord, I am sorry that my character and behavior have caused me
so many troubles.
Lord, I have made several efforts to change my ways and manner
of doing things,
But all efforts seem to be in vain.
Now I surrender my life, my body, my mind, my language to You.
O Lord, my Savior, deliver my soul and spirit from satanic control
and manipulation.
O Lord, save me from procrastination.
Please forgive me and erase my sins with the blood that was shed
on the cross.
Dear Lord, I plunge myself into the blood that was shed for me.
Let Your blood wash me, cleanse me, and set me free today
So this very moment, my whole life and being will be transformed.
O Lord God, You are the potter and I am the clay.
O Lord, turn me over into clay.
Break me, melt me, and remold me into Your original image.
Take away from me the stony heart,
And give me the heart of flesh.
Help me walk in Your will and obey Your statutes,
Line upon line and precept upon precept.
Fill me with Your likeness
That I may walk Your walk and talk Your talk,
That all who see me will see Jesus Christ, my Lord and Savior,
That no one will hear me but rather You,
That instead of offense, they will feel Your love.
Instead of insult, they will experience Your kindness.
Thank You, Lord, for delivering me from evil.
As I repent from the corrupted lifestyle that has devoured me,
I believe that you have forgiven me and set me free.
Thank You, Lord, for granting me pardon by the shedding of blood
And Your death on the cross of Calvary.

In Jesus' name, I receive total freedom and I am delivered.
Amen!

Invite the Presence of the Lord
Spirit of the living God,
Fall afresh on me.
Even as I have repented and You have forgiven me of my sins,
Lord Jesus, release the spirit of correction and instruction on me.
Yes, Lord, grant me the spirit of conviction,
That I may know when I sin against the Holy Spirit.
Please, Lord, enable me to repent and change my ways instantly
When I am convicted of sin.
Please, Lord, let me not blame others for my weakness
But rather seek to repent and change my ways.
Thank You, Lord, for renewing my spirit
And filling my life with Your presence.
Amen!

Warfare and Confrontation
Now, you evil spirit of offenses that used to influence my life,
I come against you in the name of Jesus.
The Lord has forgiven me of my sins.
The Lord has set me free from your control.
Jesus Christ is now my Lord and Savior.
Jesus Christ has shed his blood to redeem me from sin;
Therefore I am no longer under the control of sin.
I am no longer held in bondage of offenses.
Go away from me in the name of Jesus Christ.
You are no longer my friend.
Get away from me in the name of Jesus.
You are no longer my host.
I release you from my life and character.
Go out of my behavior and attitude.
I command the tree of offense built into my life, soul, and body
To be uprooted right now—in the name of Jesus.
I command the tree of offense to be uprooted
Out of my life right now—in the name of Jesus.
I command the tree that attracts sin into my life

To be uprooted right now—in the name of Jesus.
I command the fire of the Holy Spirit to consume
Every tree that has been uprooted out of my life.
I command the fire of the Holy Spirit to consume
The tree of evil that corrupts and defiles.
The blood of Jesus raises a standard against you.
The blood of Jesus builds a boundary between you and me.
You shall not see me again and I shall not invite you.
Go, go, go, and go away from me—in the name of Jesus Christ,
Who died to set me free, and I declare that I am free indeed.
Amen!

Motivational Song of Victory

"And Can It Be That I Should Gain"
Words: Charles Wesley, *Psalms and Hymns,* 1738
Music: "Sagina," Thomas Campbell, *Bouquet,* 1825

> And can it be that I should gain
> An interest in the Savior's blood?
> Died He for me, who caused His pain—
> For me, who Him to death pursued?
> Amazing love! How can it be,
> That Thou, my God, shouldst die for me?
> Amazing love! How can it be,
> That Thou, my God, shouldst die for me?
>
> 'Tis mystery all: th'Immortal dies:
> Who can explore His strange design?
> In vain the firstborn seraph tries
> To sound the depths of love divine.
> 'Tis mercy all! Let earth adore,
> Let angel minds inquire no more.
> 'Tis mercy all! Let earth adore;
> Let angel minds inquire no more.
>
> He left His Father's throne above
> So free, so infinite His grace—
> Emptied Himself of all but love,
> And bled for Adam's helpless race:

'Tis mercy all, immense and free,
For O my God, it found out me!
'Tis mercy all, immense and free,
For O my God, it found out me!

Long my imprisoned spirit lay,
Fast bound in sin and nature's night;
Thine eye diffused a quickening ray—
I woke, the dungeon flamed with light;
My chains fell off, my heart was free,
I rose, went forth, and followed Thee.
My chains fell off, my heart was free,
I rose, went forth, and followed Thee.

Still the small inward voice I hear,
That whispers all my sins forgiven;
Still the atoning blood is near,
That quenched the wrath of hostile Heaven.
I feel the life His wounds impart;
I feel the Savior in my heart.
I feel the life His wounds impart;
I feel the Savior in my heart.

No condemnation now I dread;
Jesus, and all in Him, is mine;
Alive in Him, my living Head,
And clothed in righteousness divine,
Bold I approach th'eternal throne,
And claim the crown, through Christ my own.
Bold I approach th'eternal throne,
And claim the crown, through Christ my own.

Prayer Observations and Experiences

Write down your observations and experiences as you say this prayer.

You may remember your dreams and some past occurrences while you are saying it. You may also receive a revelation. It is important that you make notes for future reference.

Observations

_____

_____

_____

_____

_____

Experiences

_____

_____

_____

_____

_____

Chapter Five

Prayer of Rededication: Reassuring Love Relationship

Rededication: There are times when people lose their passion and affection because of a situation that overwhelms them. The loss of passion and affection weakens the environment of love, and you will not have anything to share with another. To regain what has been lost, you need to reconnect and rededicate your heart through purging and cleansing. Love needs constant reassurance and rededication to stand strong.

The Prayer: If you have accepted Jesus Christ into your life, but have not been walking and living with Him according to the scriptures, then you need to rededicate your life today for reconnection. The prayer of rededication will enable you to renew your covenant of salvation, and also renew your relationship with Him. Sometimes, you may still be active in your ministry, yet you are depressed and unhappy inside. Sometimes, you condescend to sin because you are tired and disappointed. Everything seems to be on the wrong side of life. When things were not in order, you opened your spiritual door and the enemy gained access to your life and kingdom. It is time to repent and rededicate your entire life to the Lord. Invite Him to return to you. This prayer will help you regain your relationship and start afresh.

Note Page

Strategic Solution Prayer to Reconnect with Commitment and Dedication

The Problem
I need to rededicate my life to the Lord.

The Situation
My Christian life is not up to standard.
I have not been able to manage my love life with the Lord.
I have not been able to manage the Christian lifestyle.
I have not been able to maintain the presence of the Holy Spirit in my life.
I have not been able to read or study the scriptures, although I am active in church.
I have not been able to pray on my own, although I am one of the leaders in our fellowship.

The Goals
I will renew my relationship with the Lord.
I will reconnect with the environment of love.
I will be truthful and faithful in my walk with the Lord.

The Authority of Scripture
Malachi 3:7, Romans 8:1–5

Malachi 3:7
Even from the days of your fathers ye are gone away from mine ordinances, and have not kept them. Return unto me, and I will return unto you, saith the Lord of hosts. But ye said, Wherein shall we return?

Romans 8:1–5
There is therefore now no condemnation to them which are in Christ Jesus, who walk not after the flesh, but after the Spirit. For the law of the Spirit of life in Christ Jesus hath made me free from the law of sin and death. For what the law could not do, in that it was weak through the flesh, God sending his own Son in the likeness of sinful flesh, and for sin, condemned sin in the flesh: That the righteousness of the law might be fulfilled in us, who walk not after the flesh, but after the Spirit. For they that are after the flesh do mind the things of the flesh; but they that are after the Spirit the things of the Spirit.

Prayer in Action
(Praise, Worship, and Adoration)
Lord Jesus Christ, my Savior and Redeemer,
I stand before You at this hour to repent of my sins,
To ask for forgiveness of my transgression,
And to rededicate my life unto You.
I lay my life on the altar of life.
As I surrender my all to You at this moment,
I recognize the shedding of blood for the redemption of my soul
And that You died to pay the price for my sin
And to buy my pardon.
Lord, I am sorry for having wandered far away into sin.
Lord, I am coming home.
Lord Jesus, open now Your arms of love to receive me.
O Lord, like the prodigal son, I ask you to receive me,
As I return home to You.
Receive me, Lord.
Lord, your Word declares,
"For the law of the Spirit of life in Christ Jesus

has made me free from the law of sin."
Therefore deliver me from sin today.
Let Your blood wash away my sins.
Let Your blood cleanse me from all unrighteousness.
Let Your blood make me whole again,
For Your Word declares,
"For God sent not His son into the world to condemn the world,
But that the world through Him might be saved."
Therefore, I trust my life into Your hands this day,
That I might be saved from sin.
Deliver me from the works of the flesh.
Impart Your spirit into me.
Teach me to walk in the light of Your Word,
That Your Word will be a light to my path
And a lamp to my feet.
Dear Lord, transform me
By the renewal of my mind,
That I may prove myself in the light of what is good
And acceptable in Your sight.
Help me, Lord, to conform to Your perfect will.
In the name of Jesus Christ, I ask for the
Rededication of my life
As I present myself on the altar of life this day.
Amen!

Environmental Protection
In the name of Jesus,
And with the authority in the blood of Jesus,
I cover my rededication with the blood of Jesus.
I plunge my life into the blood of Jesus Christ, my Redeemer,
And seal my life with the blood of Jesus Christ.
The devil cannot stand against the blood of Jesus
That was shed for me.
The blood of Jesus speaks louder than the blood of Abel;
Therefore I am covered and sealed in the blood of Jesus
Against satanic defilement and corruption.

Warfare and Confrontation

Satan, the blood of Jesus Christ is against you.
You shall no longer influence my life.
The blood of Jesus Christ, my Redeemer, sets me free.
You shall no longer interfere with me.
The blood of Jesus Christ, my Savior, raises a standard against you.
You shall no longer harass me.
The blood of Jesus Christ delivers me.
You shall no longer terrorize my life.
In the name of Jesus, go away from me.
I command you to go out of my life.
In the name of Jesus, go out of my soul and spirit.
In the name of Jesus, go out of my body and environment.
In the name of Jesus, go out of my behavior and character.
In the name of Jesus, go out of my character.
In the name of Jesus, go out of my home and family.
Let the fire of the Holy Ghost consume your works—in Jesus' name.
Let the fire of the Holy Ghost consume
Any satanic covenant that exists between you and me—in the name
of Jesus.
You shall not visit me again and I shall not see you—in the name
of Jesus.
Let the blood of Jesus build a wall of protection around me
And a boundary against you—in the name of Jesus. Amen!

Declaration of Solution

In the name of Jesus, and with the authority in the blood of Jesus,
I declare and decree the manifestation of the word of God upon my life.
I speak to my soul and spirit to listen to the Word of the Lord
And to respond to the commands of the Lord;
I command my soul and spirit to yield the divine instructions
And to follow divine guidelines as I rededicate my life unto the
Lord this day.
I declare and decree that my soul and spirit shall resist the works of
the flesh.
I shall no longer submit to immoral activities.
I declare and decree that I shall be committed to the Word of God,

And I shall be dedicated to my vows to love the Lord with all that I am and have.

I declare and decree that I shall no longer serve two masters and I shall not be double minded in my relationship with the Lord.

Thank You, Lord, for hearing my prayers. Amen!

Motivational Song of Victory

"I've Wandered Far Away from God"
Words and Music: William J. Kirkpatrick, *Winning Songs*
(Philadelphia: John J. Hood, 1892)

I've wandered far away from God,
Now I'm coming home;
The paths of sin too long I've trod,
Lord, I'm coming home.

Refrain
Coming home, coming home,
Nevermore to roam,
Open wide Thine arms of love,
Lord, I'm coming home.

I've wasted many precious years,
Now I'm coming home;
I now repent with bitter tears,
Lord, I'm coming home.
Refrain

I'm tired of sin and straying, Lord,
Now I'm coming home;
I'll trust Thy love, believe Thy Word,
Lord, I'm coming home.
Refrain

My soul is sick, my heart is sore,
Now I'm coming home;
My strength renew, my hope restore,
Lord, I'm coming home.
Refrain

My only hope, my only plea,
Now I'm coming home;
That Jesus died, and died for me.
Lord, I'm coming home.
Refrain

I need His cleansing blood, I know,
Now I'm coming home;
O wash me whiter than the snow,
Lord, I'm coming home.
Refrain

Prayer Observations and Experiences

Write down your observations and experiences as you say this prayer.

You may remember your dreams and some past occurrences while you are saying it. You may also receive a revelation. It is important that you make notes for future reference.

Observations

_____

_____

_____

_____

_____

Experiences

_____

_____

_____

_____

_____

Part 3

The Progressive Love Life

Chapter Six

Progressiveness: Growing Love

Progress

Progress means "advancement." It means to move forward toward a goal, a target, or a destination. For there to be progress, there needs to be action. An action promotes progress because there is a process of continuity and consistency in the movement of that action.

Progress also means "growth or development." A business tends to grow because the workers are in active service or production. Where this is lacking, there is no progress. Progress is activated in the realm of laboring with dedication and commitment. Progress advances into progressiveness when action is backed with effectiveness. Whenever progress is respected, it grows into progressiveness. When progress is disrespected, it stalls into stagnancy.

Progress is a steady act of improvement that causes a person or a thing to rise from a lower level to a higher height. Where there is no growth, there will be stagnancy. Where there is no development, there will be retrogression.

Progressiveness is a dimension that can be attained in every aspect of human existence, because God deals with mankind in a progressive fashion. Hence, there are different types of progressions that can lead to progressiveness.

Spiritual Realm: In the spiritual realm, the work of the Holy Spirit is progressive; therefore, anything associated with the Lord God Almighty is likely to experience a process of progression. God created the heaven and the earth in a progressive manner. He made one thing at a time with each day. As the days went by, each element of nature was called into existence. In the beginning, God created the light in a progressive manner. First of all, He allowed the Holy Spirit to take a position that would coordinate His utterances. Then He called forth the light. When the light came forth, God looked at it, examined the sphere of its effectiveness, and saw that it was good. Then God separated the light from the darkness. Also, God advanced further in the work of creating the light by giving it a name that would distinguish it from darkness. Hence, He called the light *day* and the darkness he called *night* (Genesis 1:1–5).

Academic Realm: In the academic realm, educational programs are planned in a manner that enables a student to study in progressive steps. Children start school at nursery level (preschool) and are promoted to kindergarten. Because they are expected to learn within the environment of their understanding, children do not jump from nursery to elementary, but go through the kindergarten process, where they are given the opportunity to develop their learning abilities. Having graduated from kindergarten to primary or elementary school, children advance to middle school, where the concept of learning is fashioned in a manner that fits the age and developmental ability of teenagers. Hence, children grouped in a particular class of learning are peers of the same age group and of similar biological growth with regard to development of the human brain.

The early stages of learning are the fundamental level of education that every person is expected to achieve by age sixteen to eighteen. After the high school level of basic education, the choice of going to college or university is a unique advancement that depends on the individual's desire to go into the future. The ability to further one's education is a higher progression that can be classified as a promotion to a higher realm in life.

In continuing one's academic studies, progressiveness is a steady manner of doing things step by step to gain advancement. Since the work of the Holy Spirit is progressive, human beings should not live in the realm of deception, where all expectations are focused on instant manifestation or fulfillment without a process. When we pray, we should expect our prayer to go through a process of sowing, germinating, growing, flourishing, sprouting, and fruit bearing.

Sometimes, when our sowing is done at the right season, we harvest sooner than expected. Likewise, if our seed is a type of a cash crop like a cocoa tree that takes years to mature before bearing fruit, it will be a lasting product that will endure the times and seasons of challenges over a period of time.

Therefore, when you pray with dedication and consistency, you will reap your harvest in due season. Never give up, but know that the seed you are sowing may go through the challenges of weather conditions. Yet you shall survive, because the Lord will surely answer you. Though the answer may tarry, the Lord will see you through. However, no matter what the situation may be, your prayer shall be answered. Therefore expect instant manifestations and miracles.

Beloved, rest assured that there is instant response to your prayers and that the Lord has released legions of angels to attend to your needs. God has a spare part to replace anything that the enemy has destroyed. He has given you authority to repossess anything that has been stolen from you. The Lord has set up a watchman to watch over you even as He Himself has set His eyes upon your life. God has a purpose of prosperity for you, because of His divine purpose to make you wealthy as His blessings make you rich.

Decree this prayer with dedication and consistency. You will find things in place by the end of three months.

I shall carry my pregnancy to maturity in Jesus' name.

My pregnancy shall not suffer satanic interference—in the name of Jesus.

My pregnancy shall not be seen by the enemy—in the name of Jesus.

The enemy shall not listen to my prayers—in the name of Jesus.

The enemy shall not hear the prosperity of my prayers—in the name of Jesus.

The enemy shall not fight against my prayers—in the name of Jesus.

As you say the prayers on progressiveness,

The Lord shall hear your cry.

You shall progress to the next level in the name of Jesus Christ, our Lord and Savior. Amen!

Note Page

_____

_____

_____

_____

_____

_____

_____

_____

_____

_____

_____

_____

_____

_____

_____

_____

_____

_____

Strategic Solution Prayer
to
Experience Promotion in My Life and Daily Endeavors

The Problem
I need elevation in my life and daily endeavors.

The Situation
Everything in my life seems to be stagnant.
I have not been able to get a job in the area of my qualifications.
Every plan that I make has not materialized.
I feel as though I am just standing in the same place
and going around in circles.

The Goals
Whatever I lay my hands on to do shall prosper.
I need a change in my life and endeavors.

The Authority of Scripture
Proverbs 4:18
But the path of the just is as the shining light, that shineth more
and more unto the perfect day.

Prayer in Action
(Praise, Worship, and Adoration)
O Lord, my God,
King of Kings and Lord of lords,

Jehovah Jireh, Jehovah Nissi,
The God of creation,
The God of humanity,
Your name is to be praised and adored.
You are worthy to be praised.
Lord, I come before You at this hour to present
My petition before You.
Lord, my life has been in stagnancy.
I have not been able to make progress in my daily endeavors.
Everything seems to go around in circles.
I feel as though I have been tied down to a pillar.
I feel a barrier of limitation around my life.
Dear Lord, you are my Savior and Deliverer.
Jesus, you are my firm foundation.
Lord, Your Word says that
"the path of the just is as the shining light,
that shineth more and more unto the perfect day."
Therefore I ask that You brighten my path this day, O Lord.
Let Your light shine upon my life, O Lord,
So that the spirit of darkness will not have dominion over my life.
O Lord, You are the foundation of light, the bright and morning star.
Release me from darkness,
That I will no longer be tied down to any satanic foundation.
In You do I have my trust and protection.
Lord, release my life from any false security.
You came to set the captive free.
Lord, let not the enemy hold me in demonic bondage.
You died on the cross for my sake,
That the yoke of curses might be broken.
O Lord, let the yoke of curses be broken from my life.
By your death, You took away shame, disgrace, and
embarrassment.
O Lord, do not let the curse of shame and disgrace settle with me.
Have mercy upon me.
O Lord, my Savior and Redeemer,
Stretch forth Your hands of deliverance over me
And deliver me from stagnancy.
Release my daily endeavors

From satanic oppression and suppression.
Destroy any curse that is militating against my progress,
That I would be free to praise your name
And be able to enjoy my salvation.
O Lord, hear my cry as I lift up my head unto your hills,
From whence comes my salvation and redemption.
My help comes from You, my Lord and Savior.
Let the power of the blood
That You shed on the cross of Calvary
Deliver me from evil this day
As You delivered Daniel from the lion's den.
Open the prison gate and set me free
As You set Peter free from prison.
Break forth the shell of stagnancy from around me,
That I will be able to move up in life.
O Lord, my God,
Your Word says that with You all things are possible;
Therefore, I believe that You will deliver me from stagnancy this day.
Thank You for hearing my prayer.
Thank You for stretching forth Your hands of deliverance
To release me from satanic imprisonment.
Thank You, my Lord and Deliverer.
In Jesus' name I pray.
Amen!

Environmental Protection
In the name of Jesus,
And with the authority in the blood of Jesus,
I cover *my life and daily endeavors* with the blood of Jesus.
I plunge *my life* into the blood of Jesus Christ, my Redeemer.
I seal my life with the blood of Jesus Christ.
The devil cannot stand against the blood of Jesus
That was shed for me.
The blood of Jesus speaks louder than the blood of Abel.
Therefore I am covered and sealed in the blood of Jesus
Against satanic defilement and corruption.
I shall no longer be held in satanic imprisonment—
Because of the blood of Jesus.

Warfare and Confrontation

In the name of Jesus Christ, my Lord and Savior,
I stand under the covering of
The blood of Jesus Christ, my Redeemer,
To stand against you rulers of darkness,
Powers and principalities of darkness,
Satanic cohorts and workers of iniquity,
To declare the Lord Jesus Christ
As the light and foundation of my life.
In the name of Jesus,
I release the blood of Jesus against you.
You shall no longer haunt my life.
In the name of Jesus Christ,
I release the fire of the Holy Ghost against your stronghold.
I command any prison gate in my life
To open right now in the name of Jesus.
I command the forces of darkness
That cause me to go around in circles
To break loose right now—in the name of Jesus.
I command the evil spirit that rotates my life
In circles to be uprooted right now—in the name of Jesus.
I command the blood of Jesus Christ to destroy
The handwriting of ordinances meant
Against me right now—in the name of Jesus.
Listen to me, you evil spirit of shame and disgrace,
In the name of Jesus, I command you to go away from me.
In the name of Jesus, I evacuate you out of my life.
In the name of Jesus, I evict you and terminate your works and endeavors.
Out of my soul and out of my spirit,
Out of my body and out of my life,
Out of my body and out of my spirit.
You shall no longer harass
And embarrass me—in the name of Jesus.
You shall no longer cause me to go around in circles—in the name
of Jesus.
Let the fire of the Holy Ghost destroy the works of flesh in my life.
Let the fire of the Holy Ghost
Consume the activities of the enemy in my life.

Declaration of Solutions
The Word of the Lord says,
"But the path of the just is as the shining light,
that shineth more and more unto the perfect day."
Therefore the spirit of darkness
Shall no longer interfere with me.
I declare that my life shall be like a shining light.
No longer will my life endeavors be tied down
To satanic strongholds—in the name of Jesus.
No longer will I be held in bondage—in the name of Jesus.
No longer will I be a failure or disappointment—in the name of Jesus.
No longer will shame and disgrace
torment my life—in the name of Jesus.
The blood of Jesus Christ set me free and I am free indeed.
There is power in the blood of Jesus Christ.
I worship and adore the authority in the blood of Jesus Christ.
I praise and worship the power in the blood of Jesus Christ.
Thank you, Lord, for releasing Your power and light to shine on me,
So that I can stand against satanic cohorts.
Thank you, Lord, for the manifestation of the power of
redemption upon my life.
In Jesus' name I pray.
Amen!

Motivational Song of Victory

"There Is Power in the Blood"
Words and Music: Lewis E. Jones, 1899

Would you be free from the burden of sin?
There's power in the blood, power in the blood;
Would you o'er evil a victory win?
There's wonderful power in the blood.

Refrain
There is power, power, wonder working power
In the blood of the Lamb;
There is power, power, wonder working power
In the precious blood of the Lamb.

Would you be free from your passion and pride?
There's power in the blood, power in the blood;
Come for a cleansing to Calvary's tide;
There's wonderful power in the blood.
Refrain

Would you be whiter, much whiter than snow?
There's power in the blood, power in the blood;
Sin stains are lost in its life giving flow.
There's wonderful power in the blood.
Refrain

Would you do service for Jesus your King?
There's power in the blood, power in the blood;
Would you live daily His praises to sing?
There's wonderful power in the blood.

"Spirit of the Living God"
Words: Daniel Iverson (1926)
Music: Daniel Iverson (1926)

Spirit of the living God, fall afresh on me
Spirit of the living God, fall afresh on me
Break me, melt me, mold me, fill me
Spirit of the living God, fall afresh on me

Prayer Observations and Experiences

Write down your observations and experiences as you say this prayer.

You may remember your dreams and some past occurrences while you are saying it. You may also receive a revelation. It is important that you make notes for future reference.

Observations

_____

_____

_____

_____

_____

Experiences

_____

_____

_____

_____

_____

Chapter Seven

Progressive Prayer Life: Empowering Love

A person's life is considered progressive if he or she is focused and steadfast in his or her relationship with the Lord. Steadfast people are not easily swayed or discouraged by situations and circumstances that may confront their daily endeavor.

Prayer is a major communicative channel that you need to maintain in order to keep a relationship fresh and active. Without prayer, you have no access to the Almighty God, the Creator. Lack of prayer closes the door against you.

For instance, a home is supposed to be the foremost environment of love in our lives. Therefore, one needs to learn to share pleasantries with everyone, young and old, including the babies. Even the fetus in the womb that is being expected into the family needs communicative attention to feel welcomed and accepted before birth.

Therefore, take a step toward improving your prayer life to keep your access to God active.

Note Page

_____

_____

_____

_____

_____

_____

_____

_____

_____

_____

_____

_____

_____

_____

_____

Strategic Solution Prayer for Advancement in My Prayer life

A progressive prayer life is a progressive love life, where there is constant communication flow without unnecessary interferences and misunderstandings.

The Problem
I need progress in my prayer life.

The Situation
My prayer life is poor and ineffective.
I can pray only with people but cannot spend time in prayer by myself.
I fall asleep easily or feel tired whenever I start to pray on my own.
I feel choked or drowsy whenever I start to pray on my own.
I feel someone standing over me when I am praying.
I hear funny noises when I go into prayer.

The Goals
The Lord will teach me to pray effectively.
I will no longer suffer satanic interferences during prayer.
My heart, spirit, and body will be quickened to pray.
The Lord will stir up His divine purpose in my heart to pray effectively.
My ears will be connected to the heart of God.

The Authority of Scripture
Luke 18:1
And he spake a parable unto them to this end, that men ought always to pray, and not to faint.

Prayer in Action
(Praise, Worship, and Adoration)
Be unto the Most Holy God.
O Lord, my God,
You are the King of Glory, Jehovah God.
You are the Alpha and Omega, the beginning and the end.
You are the rock of ages, the ancient of days.
There is no God like You.
Jehovah God, there is no God like You.
Praise be to Your Holy and wonderful name.
You are worthy to be praised. Amen!
Lord, I come into Your presence to repent of my prayerlessness.
Lord, Your Word says that
"men ought always to pray, and not to faint."

Therefore I ask that You fill me with the spirit of prayer,
That I may be able to pray without ceasing.
I have come to ask forgiveness for disconnecting myself from Your communication flow.
Lord, I am sorry that I have not been in prayer and have not spent time in Your presence.
Please, Lord, forgive me and draw me closer with the cord of love.
Lord, as Your Word commands us to pray without ceasing,
Lord, teach me how to tithe my time with You in prayer.
Fill me with Your spirit of prayer
So it will motivate me to stay longer in Your presence,
So that I may have fellowship with You,
That I may hear when You speak to me, O Lord, my God.
Enable me to be like a child and follow Your directions and obey instructions
When You call me into Your presence to pray.
O Lord, deliver me from prayerlessness.

Set my spirit free that I may be able to praise Your name.
Grant me Your presence that I may be able to connect with You,
For without Your presence I cannot pray and praise You.
Without Your motivation I have no words or language to offer
thanksgiving unto You.
Lord Jesus, help me and refill me with the words and
Languages of prayer and praise this day.
O that I may find favor of communication flow before You,
The Great God of wonders.
In Jesus' name I pray.
Amen!

Environmental Protection
In the name of Jesus,
And with the authority in the blood of Jesus,
I cover my prayer life with the blood of Jesus.
I plunge my life into the blood of Jesus Christ, my Redeemer,
And seal my prayer life with the blood of Jesus Christ.
The devil will no longer stand against my prayers,
Because of the blood of Jesus
That was shed for me.
The blood of Jesus speaks louder and better than the blood of Abel.
Therefore my prayer life is covered and sealed in the blood of Jesus
Against satanic defilement and corruption.

Warfare and Confrontation
Hey Satan! Listen to me.
You shall no longer interfere with my prayer life.
I come against the spirit of prayerlessness.
In the name of Jesus, I bind you, spirit of prayerlessness,
With the blood of Jesus.
In the name of Jesus, I cast you out of my life
And throw you out into the Dead Sea.
You shall remain in the Dead Sea
Until your judgment day.
I shall not entertain you
And you shall not visit me again—in the name of Jesus.
The blood of Jesus Christ builds a wall of boundary

Between you and me.
In the name of Jesus,
Go out of my body, soul, and spirit.
Go out of my character, behavior, and attitude.
You shall no longer have access to me—in the name of Jesus.

Declaration of Solutions
The Word of the Lord says that
"men ought always to pray, and not to faint."
Therefore I stand on the Word of the Lord
To declare that I shall pray without ceasing.
I shall not allow myself to be weak.
I shall be strong in prayer.
I shall no longer be prayerless.
I shall be prayerful.
I plug my spirit into the realms of prayer.
I connect myself into the heart of God
To declare that from now onward
I shall pray effectively,
And my prayers shall rise up unto the Lord.
And the Lord shall hear my cry,
And He shall answer me.
In the name of Jesus Christ, my Lord and Savior, I pray.
Amen!

Motivational Song of Victory

"Guide Me, O Thou Great Jehovah"
Words: William Williams, "Halleluiah" (Bristol, England: 1745)
Music: "Cwm Rhondda," John Hughes, 1907

Guide me, O Thou great Jehovah,
[or Guide me, O Thou great Redeemer]
Pilgrim through this barren land.
I am weak, but Thou art mighty;
Hold me with Thy powerful hand.
Bread of Heaven, Bread of Heaven,
Feed me till I want no more;
Feed me till I want no more.

Open now the crystal fountain,
Whence the healing stream doth flow;
Let the fire and cloudy pillar
Lead me all my journey through.
Strong Deliverer, strong Deliverer,
Be Thou still my Strength and Shield;
Be Thou still my Strength and Shield.

Lord, I trust Thy mighty power,
Wondrous are Thy works of old;
Thou deliver'st Thine from thralldom,
Who for naught themselves had sold:
Thou didst conquer, Thou didst conquer,

Sin, and Satan and the grave,
Sin, and Satan and the grave.

When I tread the verge of Jordan,
Bid my anxious fears subside;
Death of deaths, and hell's destruction,
Land me safe on Canaan's side.
Songs of praises, songs of praises,
I will ever give to Thee;
I will ever give to Thee.

Musing on my habitation,
Musing on my heav'nly home,
Fills my soul with holy longings:
Come, my Jesus, quickly come;
Vanity is all I see;
Lord, I long to be with Thee!
Lord, I long to be with Thee!

Prayer Observations and Experiences

Write down your observations and experiences as you say this prayer.

You may remember your dreams and some past occurrences while you are saying it. You may also receive a revelation. It is important that you make notes for future reference.

Observations

_____

_____

_____

_____

_____

Experiences

_____

_____

_____

_____

_____

Chapter Eight

Progressive Bible Study Life: Equipping Love

Knowledge is power. Knowledge is wisdom. Knowledge is direction. Knowledge is guidance. Knowledge is leadership. Because of lack of knowledge, people perish. How do you call God your father when you do not know Him? How are you able to communicate with the Lord when you do not know His Word? How do you call yourself a medical doctor when you have not studied medicine and have no knowledge of human anatomy?

To enjoy a love relationship, you need to study the environment in which to nurture and grow that love relationship. Studying the Word of God is like a courtship relationship, which enables you to know your intended spouse personally. Similarly, studying the Bible enables you to know Him and understand His ways. The Lord is our eternal bridegroom, to whom all Christians will be married in heaven. Therefore, we need to study in a manner that allows us to discover His characteristics and adopt His lifestyle to our inadequate behavior so that we can be like him.

Study to show yourself approved in knowledge and wisdom, and you will be confident in what you say or do.

2 Timothy 2:15 Study to shew thyself approved unto God, a workman that needeth not to be ashamed, rightly dividing the word of truth.

Hosea 4:6 My people are destroyed for lack of knowledge: because thou hast rejected knowledge, I will also reject thee, that thou shalt be no priest to me: seeing thou hast forgotten the law of thy God, I will also forget thy children.

Note Page

Strategic Solution Prayer for Equipment and Empowerment to Love the Word of God

The Problem
I need to progress in Bible studies.

The Situation
My Bible study life is poor.
When I read the Bible on my own, I hardly understand what I have read.
Sometimes I feel someone is trying to take the Bible away from me when I want to read.
I fall asleep easily or feel tired whenever I start to read the Bible, but I don't feel the same way when reading novels or other books.
I feel choked or drowsy whenever I start to read loudly in order not to fall asleep.
I feel someone standing over me when I am reading.
I hear funny noises and sometimes voices whenever I am reading the Bible.

The Goals
The Lord will grant me understanding in the Word.
I will no longer suffer satanic interferences during Bible studies.
My heart, soul, and body will be quickened to study scripture.
The Lord will stir up His divine purpose in my heart to study the scripture.
My ears will be connected to the heart of God.

The Authority of Scripture
2 Timothy 2:15, Hosea 4:6

2 Timothy 2:15
Study to shew thyself approved unto God, a workman that
needeth not to be ashamed, rightly dividing the word of truth.

Hosea 4:6
My people are destroyed for lack of knowledge: because thou hast
rejected knowledge, I will also reject thee, that thou shalt be no
priest to me: seeing thou hast forgotten the law of thy God, I will
also forget thy children.

Prayer in Action
(Praise, Worship, and Adoration)
O Lord Most Holy,
The God of Righteousness,
The all-knowing God,
The Creator and Maker of all things,
Hallowed be Your name.
You are worthy to be praised.
You are worthy of our praise.
You are the great "I Am,"
The great God of wonders,
The everlasting King of Kings.
Precious are the works of Your hands.
There is none to compare with You.
Hallelujah to the King of Glory. Amen!
Lord, I stand before you this day to apologize for my lack of studiousness.
Lord, forgive me for failing to tithe my time to study Your Word.
Scripture commands us to study to show ourselves
Approved unto God so that we would not be ashamed.
Lord, forgive me for disobeying your commands to study, to show
myself approved unto you.
Because of lack of study, I opened the door for the enemy to rob
me of the word of truth.

Hence the enemy has been able to corrupt my mind and heart
with lies and deception.
O Lord, you are the God of truth.
We perish because of lack of knowledge,
As your word also declares in Hosea 4:6 that
"My people are destroyed for lack of knowledge."
O Lord, I ask for forgiveness for rejecting Your knowledge.
Please, Lord, do not reject me,
So that I will not perish from Your sight.
Please, Lord, enable me to return to Your Word,
That I may remember your commandments
And not forget your statutes.
Please, Lord, remember me this day
And grant me the hunger for Your Word
And the thirst for your righteousness.
Thank you, Lord,
For restoring me into the study of Your Word.
Thank you, Jehovah Jireh,
For granting me the hunger for righteousness.
Thank you, Jehovah Nissi,
For stirring me up with the desire to know You more.
In the name of Jesus Christ, my Savior, I pray.
Amen!

Environmental Protection
In the name of Jesus,
And with the authority in the blood of Jesus,
I cover my Bible study life with the blood of Jesus.
I plunge my life into the blood of Jesus Christ, my Redeemer,
And seal my Bible studies with the blood of Jesus Christ.
The devil will no longer stand against my Bible studies,
Because of the blood of Jesus
That was shed for me.
The blood of Jesus speaks louder than the blood of Abel.
Therefore my Bible study life is covered and sealed in the blood of Jesus
Against satanic defilement and corruption! Amen!

Warfare and Confrontation
Hey Satan! Listen to me.
You shall no longer interfere with my Bible studies.
I come against the spirit that prohibits the knowledge of truth.
In the name of Jesus, I bind you, spirit,
That hinders the knowledge of God.
With the power in the blood of Jesus,
I uproot the spirit that causes lack of knowledge
Out of my body, soul, and spirit.
In the name of Jesus, I cast you out of my life
And throw you out into the Dead Sea.
You shall remain in the Dead Sea until your judgment day.
I shall not entertain you
And you shall not visit me again—in the name of Jesus.
The blood of Jesus Christ builds a wall of boundary
Between you and me.
In the name of Jesus, I command you to go.
Go out of my body, soul, and spirit.
Go out of my character, behavior, and attitude.
You shall no longer have access to me—in the name of Jesus.

Declaration of Solutions
The Word of the Lord commands me in 2 Timothy 2:15
To study to show myself approved unto God.
Therefore I declare that from today onward
I shall study the Word of God,
That I may know the truth,
And the truth that I study in the Scriptures
Shall cause me to prosper and I shall not fail.
Scripture also commands me
To be a workman that needs not to be ashamed.
Therefore I shall not be ashamed to study the Word of God,
And I shall not allow myself to lack knowledge
So that I will not be put to shame.
In the name of Jesus, I declare
That I will increase in the knowledge of God.
As I study the Scriptures,

I shall rightly divide the Word of truth
Into my body, soul, and spirit.
In the name of Jesus,
The knowledge of the Word of God
Shall be applicable to my environment,
In my going out and my coming in
And in all my life endeavors.
I declare that I shall not perish—in the name of Jesus.
I shall not lack knowledge—in the name of Jesus.
I shall not stay away from Bible studies—in the name of Jesus.
God will not reject me—in the name of Jesus.
The scriptures shall cause the Lord to remember me—in the name
of Jesus.
Therefore I stand on the Word of the Lord
To declare that I shall study the scriptures without ceasing.
I shall not allow myself to be weak.
I shall be strong in Bible studies.
I shall no longer be without the knowledge of God.
I shall be hungry for righteousness.
I plug my spirit into the realms of biblical knowledge.
I connect myself into the heart of God
To declare that from now onward
I shall study the Word of God effectively,
And the Word of God shall be a light to my path
And a lamp to my feet.
And the Word of the Lord shall guard and lead me
In the path of righteousness.
In the name of Jesus Christ, my Lord and Savior, I pray.
Amen!

Motivational Song of Victory

"Just a Closer Walk with Thee"
Words: Author unknown
Music: "Closer Walk," traditional folk song

> I am weak but Thou art strong
> Jesus keep me from all wrong
> I'll be satisfied as long as I walk
> Dear Lord, close to Thee.
>
> Just a closer walk with Thee
> Grant it Jesus, is my plea
> Daily walkin' close to Thee
> Let it be, dear Lord, let it be.
>
> Through this world of toils and snares
> If I falter Lord, who cares?
> Who with me my burden shares?
> None but Thee, dear Lord, none but Thee.
>
> Just a closer walk with Thee
> Grant it Jesus, is my plea
> Daily walkin' close to Thee
> Let it be, dear Lord, let it be.

When my feeble life is o'er
And time for me will be no more
Guide me gently, safely o'er
To Thy kingdom dear Lord, to Thy shore.

Just a closer walk with Thee
Grant it Jesus, is my plea
Daily walkin' close to Thee
Let it be, dear Lord, let it be.

Prayer Observations and Experiences

Write down your observations and experiences as you say this prayer.

You may remember your dreams and some past occurrences while you are saying it. You may also receive a revelation. It is important that you make notes for future reference.

Observations

_____

_____

_____

_____

_____

Experiences

_____

_____

_____

_____

_____

Chapter Nine

Progressive Spiritual life: Active Love

A person's spiritual life is a reflection of a godly relationship. If you have a personal relationship with the Lord, it will be reflected in your character and behavior. Godly behavior can never be hidden, because it takes over your whole being as though you are in love with the opposite sex. You can't refrain from talking about your lover. Your thoughts and actions are saturated with expressions of love that cannot be hidden.

If you have never experienced the love of God, you will not know how to carry Him in your bosom. If you have never fallen in love with the Lord, then you have not yet gone on a date with Him. You have also not had the opportunity to be courted.

Beloved, you need to fall in love with the Lord as a seed falls into fertile soil, so that you can germinate a passionate love for the Lord Jesus Christ. Following the germination, you will begin to grow in love. As you grow in the love of the Lord Jesus, you will be refreshed, and the joy of salvation will fill your heart and saturate your total being.

When you are in love with the Lord, you will always want to be around Him for romantic affection and passion. The moment of romance activates the need for prayer. Prayer is a romantic affair with the Lord.

The moment of affection is when you want to have a heart-to-heart conversation with the Lord. The moment of conversation motivates your Bible study life because you want to know Him more and more.

As you study the Word, you also want to enter into his bosom and feel His heart, so that you can know His desires and do His will. The desire to know the Lord plugs you into a higher voltage of electricity that connects you to a higher level of hunger and thirst for righteousness. This manner of desire connects you to prayer and intercession through fasting. If you stay plugged in and connected to the Lord at this level, your spiritual lifestyle will of course be an open book whereby you will be clothed in the righteousness of the Lord. Your lifestyle will not be a struggle with the works of the flesh, but a natural demonstration of the fruit of the spirit. Your lifestyle will be in the progressive lane and not in the struggling lane. You need to plant your life on Jesus Christ the solid rock, and you will experience the joy of knowing Him as your Lord and Savior. Then He will be the source of your joy and the strength of your existence (John 4:7–14).

Note Page

Strategic Solution Prayer
for
Active Love Life in Christ Jesus

The Problem
I need progress in my spiritual love life.

The Situation
My spiritual walk with God is not solid.
I have not been able to do what I pray for.
I have not been able to apply the scriptures to my daily lifestyle.
I have not been an example to my environment.
I often have disagreements with people.
I have not been able to maintain relationships.
I am easily motivated but always procrastinating.

The Goals
The Lord will enable me to live an active love life.
The Lord will teach me His ways.
I will no longer procrastinate.
My heart, spirit, and body will be quickened
to love the Lord in all that I say and do.
I will walk in the statutes and precepts of the Lord.
I will be conscious of God in all my endeavors.
The fear of God will come upon me to guide and lead me.
The words of my mouth and the meditation of my heart will be
influenced by His will.
The Lord will stir up His divine purpose in my heart to pray effectively.
My ears will be connected to the heart of God.

The Authority of Scripture
Genesis 1:26, Genesis 6:8–9

Genesis 1:26
And God said, Let us make man in our image, after our likeness: and let them have dominion over the fish of the sea, and over the fowl of the air, and over the cattle, and over all the earth, and over every creeping thing that creepeth upon the earth.

Genesis 6:8–9
But Noah found grace in the eyes of the Lord. These are the generations of Noah: Noah was a just man and perfect in his generations, and Noah walked with God.

Prayer in Action
(Praise, Worship, and Adoration)
O Lord, my God,
You are awesome.
You reign in heaven and on earth.
You are the omnipotent Father.
God, You reign in majesty,
You are the King of Glory.
The heavens are telling Your glory.
The earth is proclaiming the works of Your hands.
Blessed are you, O Lord.
The earth cannot contain Your glory.
We give you all the praise and adoration.
Blessed be Your name.
Precious is Your name.
Glory, honor, adoration, and praise
Be unto you. Amen!
My Lord and my Creator,
I have come into Your presence
To seek Your face,
To be restored into the original image
In which You created me.
For your Word says in Genesis 1:26 that

You created me in your image according to your likeness.
Therefore I pray, let Your image return to me, O Lord,
That I may reflect Your character.
Let Your likeness fill my spirit, O Lord,
That I may do the works that You do.
Dear Lord, enable me to walk with You
As Noah was able to demonstrate righteousness
In the midst of evil and a perverse generation
And overcome corruption.
O Lord, put Your spirit in me
That I may fear You in all my endeavors,
That I will no longer corrupt my ways
Or conform to wickedness.
Thank You, Jehovah Jireh,
For delivering me from evil.
Thank You, Jehovah Tsidkenu,
For restoring me into righteousness.
Thank You, Jehovah Shalom,
For restoring Your image and likeness in me.
Thank You, Jehovah Shammah,
For releasing Your presence over me.
This I pray, and I thank You in Jesus' name.
Amen!

Environmental Protection
In the name of Jesus,
And with the authority in the blood of Jesus,
I cover *my spiritual life* with the blood of Jesus.
I plunge *my spiritual life* into the blood of Jesus Christ, my Redeemer,
And seal my spiritual life with the blood of Jesus Christ.
The devil will no longer stand against *my relationship with the Lord*—
Because of the blood of Jesus
That was shed for me.
The blood of Jesus speaks louder and better than the blood of Abel.
Therefore *my spiritual life* is covered and sealed in the blood of Jesus
Against satanic defilement and corruption. Amen!

Warfare and Confrontation

In the name of Jesus,
I bind the spirit of interruption and corruption
That used to influence my life.
With the authority in the blood of Jesus,
I command the spirit of interruption and corruption to be
uprooted out of my life.
In the name of Jesus, I cast out the uprooted spirit from my life.
I command you, spirit of interruption
And corruption, to go into Gahanna right now.
I evacuate you out of my life, out of my body,
Out of my soul, and out of my spirit.
I issue you an eviction notice.
You shall no longer operate in my life.
You shall no longer have access to my spirit,
soul, and body—in the name of Jesus.
I am washed in the blood of Jesus Christ, my Redeemer.
Therefore I shut the door with the blood of Jesus Christ against you.
The blood of Jesus builds
A wall of boundary between you and me.
You shall not see me again and I shall not invite you—
Because of the blood of Jesus
Amen!

Declaration of Solutions

In the name of Jesus, I release myself from the devil,
And I establish a new relationship in Christ Jesus.
The Word of God says
Old things shall pass away and new things shall come;
Therefore I declare a new relationship in my life
Right now in the name of Jesus.
I declare a new destiny of relationship in Christ Jesus.
I call forth the image of God to replace
The corrupted image that has gone out of me—
In the name of Jesus.
I plant the image of God into my character.

In the name of Jesus, I adopt the likeness of God
Into my heart and abilities.
In the name of Jesus, I declare the blessings of
the Most High God, my Creator, upon my life.
In Jesus' name, I am free and released.
In Jesus' name, I have a new relationship with the Lord.
Amen!

Motivational Song of Victory

"Teach Me Thy Way, O Lord"
Words: Benjamin M. Ramsey, 1919
Music: "Camacha," Benjamin M. Ramsey

Teach me Thy way, O Lord, teach me Thy way!
Thy guiding grace afford, teach me Thy way!
Help me to walk aright, more by faith, less by sight;
Lead me with heav'nly light, teach me Thy way!

When I am sad at heart, teach me Thy way!
When earthly joys depart, teach me Thy way!
In hours of loneliness, in times of dire distress,
In failure or success, teach me Thy way!

When doubts and fears arise, teach me Thy way!
When storms o'erspread the skies, teach me Thy way!
Shine through the cloud and rain, through sorrow, toil
and pain;
Make Thou my pathway plain, teach me Thy way!

Long as my life shall last, teach me Thy way!
Where'er my lot be cast, teach me Thy way!
Until the race is run, until the journey's done,
Until the crown is won, teach me Thy way!

Prayer Observations and Experiences

Write down your observations and experiences as you say this prayer.

You may remember your dreams and some past occurrences while you are saying it. You may also receive a revelation. It is important that you make notes for future reference.

Observations

_____

_____

_____

_____

_____

Experiences

_____

_____

_____

_____

_____

Part 4

The Secular Endeavors

Chapter Ten

Progressive Academic Endeavors

Are you a brilliant student experiencing examination failure? Are you a hardworking student and yet cannot make headway in your life?

Are you struggling with your studies?

Are you struggling with academic progress?

Are you struggling with everything that is related to schoolwork and life?

Whatever the struggles are, there are always solutions. If your academic struggle is related to a curse, this prayer will help you.

If your academic weakness is related to poverty, this prayer will give you a step through an open door.

If your academic challenge is related to a mysterious interference, this prayer will expose evil ordinances written against you.

Whatever the problem may be, call upon the name of the Lord Jesus Christ, and cry unto Him. He will hear and answer you. Prayer is the key that opens the door to every destiny.

My Academic Challenges: As a result of the witchcraft attack that Madam Ruthie launched against me when she posed as a babysitter for my mum, I had trouble with my academic endeavors. During examination periods, I suffered from headaches and blankness in my mind, which resulted in failures and disappointments. My head would start to ache so badly that I would not be able to think of anything or understand the questions before me. In view of the challenges that I experienced with my academic shortfalls and failure, I found a deeper relationship with God. I fasted and prayed to God for examination success, and He granted me favor. Failure taught me to surrender my totality to the Lord and depend on Him for everything in life.

Failure: Failure is not the end of life, but the beginning of a new discovery. Failure is not a destruction of visions, but an ignition of new innovation.

Failure is not a burial ground, but a cultivation of new life. Let a failure in one aspect of your life motivate you to discover new grounds for progress.

Let failure of an ambition propel you into fresh water to fish for ideas.

The following testimony, given by one of my protégés I will refer to as Faith, is a good example of how prayer can enable people to overcome every obstacle in their way and accomplish whatever they set set out to do.

Academic Testimony

Faith: Some students are known to be most improved, have perfect attendance, and exhibit good citizenship throughout their college years. I was the A student. I always got the best grades on homework, tests— you name it! It would be out of character for me to miss a class, which I never did. You could say I was the perfect example of a good student.

Stepping into college, also known as the "real world," and greatly overwhelmed with my parents' constant disagreements and confusion on the home front, my performance in school was affected and the A's disappeared from my identity. I took a good amount of classes as a freshman; one or two sciences here, an English class there, math and history classes—all the basic stuff. I did wonderfully well, getting used to the flow of things. I did well on class tests and exam papers.

After about three months of my adjusting to the life of a college student, my dad started pestering me to get a job, so I could assist in paying for school. My immediate thought was *How can I focus on school if my one priority, according to my dad, should be paying my way?* My mom was completely against the idea. This issue was an ongoing battle between my parents, so I went ahead and got a part-time job to cease the fire. This way, I could make a little change and still balance my classes. I took up four night shifts during the week. Within two weeks, there was a significant drop in my grades, and sleep started to pounce on me during lectures. My professors scheduled a meeting with me to ask why my grades had taken a sudden turn for the worse, and I explained why. They explained that the time I used for work should be used for studying, because it would be difficult to pass the courses if I did not give them my full concentration. I took the words of advice to my parents, but my dad stood firm in his decision for me to work. He justified himself by saying, "If I paid my way through as young as you are, so can you." My mom tried to step in as the voice of reason, but her voice fell on deaf ears.

Reaching the point of helplessness, I decided to consult with Dr. Pauline about my issue. She suggested I fast for three days and present my request before the Lord. After I had fasted, she took me into her office for counseling. She advised me to let go of the job because the money I was working for was the same money I would waste by not focusing on passing my classes, which, I might add, were not cheap. I brought my parents together and told them I would be leaving my job in order to focus on my studies, and would take up employment whenever school was not in session.

Although my father was not happy with my decision, he and my mother were happy to see that my grades were back up to where they had been. I finished the semester with exceptional success and found myself a summer job. I was able to save up and pay for a portion of the school fees. Everyone was pleased with the result, and all glory and honor was given to God. I give special thanks to Dr. Pauline Walley-Daniels, who did not turn me away in my time of despair.

The above testimony is a good example of how money can be an impediment to the academic progression of one's life.

The following prayer will cause you to rise above the failure that causes stagnation.

Note Page

Strategic Solution Prayer
for
Academic Success

The Problem
I need to progress in my studies and career.

The Situation
I have not been doing well with my studies.
I easily forget during examinations.
I have difficulty understanding questions.

The Goals
The Lord will bless me with the spirit of Daniel.
The Lord will bless me with the spirit of excellence.

The Authority of Scripture
Daniel 1:17, Psalm 119:99

Daniel 1:17
As for these four children, God gave them knowledge and skill
in all learning and wisdom: and Daniel had understanding in all
visions and dreams.

Psalm 119:99
I have more understanding than all my teachers: for thy
testimonies are my meditation.

Prayer in Action
(Praise, Worship, and Adoration)
Father of life,
El-Elohim, Jehovah God,
Jehovah Nissi, the great conqueror,
Jehovah Shalom, the God of peace,
You are the King of Glory and the Lord of Lords.
You are the God of wisdom and knowledge.
You are the God of excellence.
Excellent is Your name, O Lord.
Excellent is Your power, Almighty God.
You are worthy to be praised and exalted.
Worship and adoration belong to You,
Great God of wonders.
Lord, I invite You into my life
And academic endeavors.
O Lord, wisdom and knowledge comes from You;
Therefore I ask that You endow me
With wisdom and knowledge,
That I may be skillful and excel
In my academic endeavors.
O Lord, the scripture says that
"God gave them knowledge and skill
in all learning and wisdom:
and Daniel had understanding
in all visions and dreams."
O Lord, impart into me the kind of ability
That you gave to Daniel,
That I may excel
In all my educational performance,
That I will be on top and never below,
That I will be above and never beneath.
O Lord, according to Your Word in Psalm 119:99,
It will be recorded that
"I have more understanding
than all my teachers,"
Because the favor of the Living God

Is with me! Amen!
Lord, I ask that You give me the motivation to study,
To show myself approved unto my examiner.
O Lord, grant me retentive memory
To remember and not forget.
O Lord, take away from me
Envy, jealousy, and strife
From among my colleagues,
That they may not hate me because of my skillfulness,
But that I will gain favor of love, acceptance,
Honor, and respect from my teachers and friends.
O Lord, surround me with Your presence
And protect me from the evil of wickedness
That might want to attack my blessings.
Thank You, Lord, for granting me
The desires of my heart.
Thank You for granting me
Wisdom and knowledge to
Excel above all requirements.
Thank You, Lord.
In Jesus' name I pray.
Amen!

Environmental Protection

In the name of Jesus,
And with the authority in the blood of Jesus,
I cover my *educational endeavors* with the blood of Jesus.
I plunge my life into the blood of Jesus Christ, my Redeemer,
And seal my academic studies with the blood of Jesus Christ.
The devil will no longer stand against my *academic endeavors*
Because of the blood of Jesus
That was shed for me.
The blood of Jesus speaks louder and better than the blood of Abel.
Therefore my *academic life* is covered and sealed in the blood of Jesus
Against satanic defilement, interference, and corruption! Amen!

Warfare and Confrontation
Satan, listen to me.
The Word of the Lord says that
Power and might belong to the Almighty God,
The King of Glory and the Maker of all things.
The Word of the Lord also says that
"God gave them knowledge and skill
in all learning and wisdom:
and Daniel had understanding
in all visions and dreams."
Therefore, you and your evil cohorts
Shall not interfere with me.
In the name of Jesus, I come against you, spirit of failure and
retrogression.
In the name of Jesus, I bind you, evil spirits
That obstruct knowledge in my academic endeavors.
In the name of Jesus, I uproot you, trees of failure,
Disappointment, retrogression, and stagnancy
That interfere with my academic endeavors.
In the name of Jesus,
I command the fire of the Holy Ghost
To destroy the root of evil planted
Against my academic destiny.
In the name of Jesus, I cast you out of my life
And send you into the Dead Sea.
In the name of Jesus, I evict any demonic influence
That wants to interrupt my educational abilities.
In the name of Jesus, I command you
To go out of my life right now.
Go out of my mind, out of abilities,
Out of my character and behavior.
The blood of Jesus destroys your works.
The fire of the Holy Ghost consumes your activities.
You shall no longer interfere with me.
You shall not come by me and I shall not invite you.
The blood of Jesus builds a wall of demarcation
Between you and me.

Go to the Dead Sea and remain there
Until your judgment day.
The blood of Jesus raises a standard against you, Satan.
In Jesus' name I pray. Amen!

Declaration of Solutions
In the name of Jesus,
I stand on the authority of scripture
To loosen my blessings
From the hand of Satan and his cohorts.
In the name of Jesus, I command
My blessing to come forth.
In the name of Jesus, I declare
Success against failure.
I declare retentive memory against forgetfulness.
I declare knowledge and wisdom
Against foolishness—in Jesus' name.
I declare progressiveness and skillfulness
Against retrogression—in Jesus' name.
I release my abilities to prosper—in Jesus' name.
I release my gifts and talents to prosper—in Jesus' name.
I declare my academic destiny to prosper—in Jesus' name.
I plant my educational destiny in the vineyard of prosperity.
I cover my academic destiny with the blood of Jesus,
And I build a hedge of protection around my life
And academic destiny—in Jesus' name.
Thank You, Lord, for fighting my battles
And granting me victory.
In Jesus' name I pray!
Amen!

Dr. Pauline Walley-Daniels

Motivational Song of Victory

"O Worship the King"
Words: Robert Grant, 1779–1838
Music: Attributed to Johann Michael Haydn, 1737–1806

O worship the King, all glorious above,
O gratefully sing God's power and God's love;
our Shield and Defender, the Ancient of Days,
pavilioned in splendor, and girded with praise.

O tell of God's might, O sing of God's grace,
whose robe is the light, whose canopy space,
whose chariots of wrath the deep thunderclouds form,
and dark is God's path on the wings of the storm.

The earth with its store of wonders untold,
Almighty, thy power hath founded of old;
hath stablished it fast by a changeless decree,
and round it hath cast, like a mantle, the sea.

Thy bountiful care, what tongue can recite?
It breathes in the air, it shines in the light;
it streams from the hills, it descends to the plain,
and sweetly distills in the dew and the rain.

Frail children of dust, and feeble as frail,
in thee do we trust, nor find thee to fail;
thy mercies how tender, how firm to the end,
our Maker, Defender, Redeemer, and Friend.

Prayer Observations and Experiences

Write down your observations and experiences as you say this prayer.

You may remember your dreams and some past occurrences while you are saying it. You may also receive a revelation. It is important that you make notes for future reference.

Observations

_____

_____

_____

_____

_____

Experiences

_____

_____

_____

_____

_____

Chapter Eleven

Progressive Business Transactions

A daily life endeavor incorporates one's business transactions. A successful business life provides for a measure of peace of mind in relation to financial resources. However, a satisfying business transaction does not guarantee a successful life and lifestyle. One needs a closer walk with God for lifelong satisfaction.

There is a need to cultivate a closer walk with the Lord, for spiritual and emotional satisfaction. Many people move out of corporate organizations to start their own businesses because they feel they have more to offer than what they were allowed to do. Some start small businesses because they want to challenge their skills and productivity without hindrance from anyone. Others start their own business because they want to break new ground and demonstrate their unique abilities. Some people have been successful and expanded their dreams beyond their primary vision and mission.

On the other hand, some people have had to struggle with their dreams and aspirations, because they have not been able to yield enough production to cover their overhead to meet their basic needs. Some initially made progress and then stalled. Hence, they are living in lack and poverty. Their daily business transaction lacks fruitfulness irrespective of the amount of investment sunk into it.

Onetime progress should be geared into progressive mode so that one's business transaction will continue to prosper in season and out of season. A progressive business transaction is the type that attracts favor from all walks of life. Prospective clients are attracted and drawn to support and invest their quota into each transaction.

Many businesspeople may not know the importance of prayer until trouble strikes. Some like to be prayed for but think it is a waste of time to get involved at a time that they should be resting or bidding for new transactions. Prayer is necessary because grace is needed to deal with certain clients. Some clients will not indulge in open prayer but would rather consult clairvoyants and diviners to assist them, using talismans and other spiritual elements. Others turn to hide their spiritual activities behind closed doors and pretend their business success is a normal thing.

Praying over a business transaction attracts success and stability against stagnancy. One should learn to fight against satanic attacks in business and also bless the name of the Lord over fruitful ventures. The following prayer language should be adopted to help influence successful business transactions.

Note Page

Strategic Solution Prayer
for
Successful Business Transactions

The Problem
I need progressiveness in my daily business transactions.

The Situation
I am unable to make enough profit.
I am unable to expand.
I am suffering from stagnancy.
I am facing competition from envy, jealousy, and strife.

The Goals
The Lord will bless me with Jacob's blessings.
The Lord will give me creativity and unique business ideas.
The Lord will bless me with excellent performance in my business endeavors.
The work of my hands will prosper.

The Authority of Scripture
Genesis 30:43

And the man increased exceedingly, and had much cattle, and maidservants, and menservants, and camels, and asses.

Prayer in Action
(*Praise, Worship, and Adoration*)
O Lord, my God,
Jehovah Jireh—the great provider,
Jehovah Shammah—the ever present God,
Jehovah Nissi—the mighty warrior,
O Lord God Almighty,
Your name represents the works of Your hands.
Your name speaks about the power of Your creation.
Your name announces Your glory.
Your name reveals Your power.
Your name be praised and exalted.
Your name be uplifted above all others.
Great God of wonders are You,
Father Lord.
Business and employment comes from you.
In the beginning You commanded mankind
To be fruitful, to multiply and replenish the earth.
O Lord, You also gave man power
To subdue the earth and have dominion
Over the birds, the cattle, and everything
In which there is life.
O Lord, in Genesis chapter two,
You also set up the Garden of Eden
And you put man in the Garden
To tend and keep it.
O Lord, my God,
Your Word also says that
He who refuses to work should not eat;
Therefore, look upon my business
And show me Your favor.
O Lord, look upon my employment
And breathe life into it.
O Lord, consider the work of Your hand
And the word that you have spoken;
To cause the dew of heaven to rain down
Upon my business and employment this day,

That I may flourish and prosper.
The enemy will not come upon me like the Midianites,
And the workers of iniquity will not rob me of my wages
As in the case of Laban and Jacob.
O Lord, I ask that you prosper my transactions.
O Lord, grant me your favor with my clients.
O Lord, bless my products and services.
Jehovah Jireh, bless the work of my hands,
That I may prosper in wealth and financial resources
And also prosper above all things.
This I pray in Jesus' name. Amen!

Environmental Protection
In the name of Jesus,
And with the authority in the blood of Jesus,
I cover my *business endeavors* and *employment* with the blood of Jesus.
I plunge my life into the blood of Jesus Christ, my Redeemer,
And seal my *business transactions and resources* with the blood of
Jesus Christ.
The devil will no longer stand against my *business life and
environment*—
Because of the blood of Jesus
That was shed for me.
The blood of Jesus speaks louder than the blood of Abel.
Therefore my *business life* is covered and sealed in the blood of Jesus
Against satanic interference, defilement, and corruption. Amen!
Let the fire of the Holy Ghost build a wall of protection
Over my business endeavors,
In the name of Jesus Christ, my Savior and Deliverer. Amen!

Warfare and Confrontation
In the name of Jesus,
And with the authority in the blood of Jesus,
I come against you, Satan.
The Word of God declares
In Genesis chapter one
That God gave the authority to make wealth to mankind.
As it is written in Genesis 1:28,

"And God blessed them,
and God said unto them,
Be fruitful, and multiply,
and replenish the earth, and subdue it."
Therefore, Satan, you and your cohorts
Shall not terrorize my business deals—in Jesus' name.
It is also written in Proverbs 12:11,
"He that tilleth his land shall be satisfied with bread."
Therefore you powers and principalities of darkness
Shall not harass my business endeavors.
In the name of Jesus, I bind the arrows of deception
That interfere with my business transactions by day
And uproot the terror of Midianites
That destroy my business resources by night.
I cast you out of my business endeavors—in the name of Jesus.
I evict you out of my business relationships—in the name of Jesus.
You shall no longer have access to my business
Endeavors—in the name of Jesus.
The blood of Jesus raises a standard against you.
You shall not see me again and you shall not interfere with
My business ventures.
The blood of Jesus builds a wall of protection
Around my business ventures.
The fire of the Holy Ghost builds
A hedge of protection around my resources.
In Jesus' name I pray.
Amen!

Declaration of Solutions

In the name of Jesus,
I stand on the authority in the Word of God
To declare blessings upon my
Business endeavors.
In the name of Jesus,
I declare and decree progressiveness in my business ventures.
In the name of Jesus,
I declare and decree profits and success in my business.
In the name of Jesus, I declare abundance

In my business life.
In the name of Jesus,
I declare and decree wealth and prosperity
In my business.
In the name of Jesus,
I declare and decree that I shall not work
For another to eat.
I declare and decree that I shall not sow
For another to reap.
I declare and decree that I shall reap the harvest of my toil.
I declare and decree that I shall enjoy the harvest of my business.
In Jesus' name I pray.
Amen!

Motivational Song of Victory

"Nearer, My God, to Thee"
Words: Sarah F. Adams, 1805–1848
Music: Lowell Mason, 1792–1872

Nearer, my God, to thee, nearer to thee!
E'en though it be a cross that raiseth me,
still all my song shall be,
nearer, my God, to thee;
nearer, my God, to thee, nearer to thee!

Though like the wanderer, the sun gone down,
darkness be over me, my rest a stone;
yet in my dreams I'd be
nearer, my God, to thee;
nearer, my God, to thee, nearer to thee!

There let the way appear, steps unto heaven;
all that thou sendest me, in mercy given;
angels to beckon me
nearer, my God, to thee;
nearer, my God, to thee, nearer to thee!

Then, with my waking thoughts bright with thy praise,
out of my stony griefs Bethel I'll raise;
so by my woes to be
nearer, my God, to thee;
nearer, my God, to thee, nearer to thee!

Or if, on joyful wing cleaving the sky,
sun, moon, and stars forgot, upward I fly,
still all my song shall be,
nearer, my God, to thee;
nearer, my God, to thee, nearer to thee!

Prayer Observations and Experiences

Write down your observations and experiences as you say this prayer.

You may remember your dreams and some past occurrences while you are saying it. You may also receive a revelation. It is important that you make notes for future reference.

Observations

_____

_____

_____

_____

_____

Experiences

_____

_____

_____

_____

_____

Chapter Twelve

Progressive Employment

Usually, one's professional endeavor is supposed to sum up one's progressive life. How one does on a job determines one's social status and satisfaction. People who earn good salaries are able to provide for their families and themselves. People who gain promotion for excellent performance will also be blessed to occupy executive positions.

A good working environment provides a blessing that is often beyond salary earning and status. If a working environment is saturated with obnoxious activities where envy, jealousy, strife, or false accusation are the order of the day, no amount of salary paid or official status can satisfy.

Progressive employment is where there is hope for everyone, room for individuals to exhibit their talents and professional ideas, and opportunity for elevation without fear of intimidation.

It is possible to go to work with joy in our hearts, use our abilities, and return home to celebrate our daily achievements, which encourages peace and satisfaction in our homes.

Progressive Employment

The following testimony, given by somebody I counseled some time ago, shows how important it is to commit all our endeavors to the hands of God through prayers. Prayer is the most important weapon we can use to foil all satanic plots and plans against our endeavors. Without prayers, we cannot progress in life, and our plans might not come to an expected end. This person's name has been changed to protect his privacy.

Roshua's Story

My name is Roshua, and I am a certified public accountant by profession. I worked for a very prestigious financial company for about eight years. I had planned to work with this company for much longer than that, and had high hopes of rising through the ranks and becoming one of the top members of the company. However, things did not work out the way I hoped they would.

Although my colleagues were very hardworking and good at their jobs, there was a lot of insecurity amongst them. Everyone was afraid someone was going to undermine them and have them fired. It seemed to be almost a pattern in the office. One had to watch whatever they said, and whom they said it to. There was so much envy and jealousy amongst us. Whenever there was a vacant position in the managerial level of the company and people applied for that position, those people received the brunt of the envy and jealousy. Even if they were not offered the position, it did not seem to matter. The fact that they had shown a desire for a higher position was enough for our colleagues to resent them and not get along well with them.

I was one of the people to apply for such a position. There was an opening for a managerial position in the accounts department, and I was really interested in it. I also had the credentials they were looking for, and was confident I would be able to do the work effectively should it be offered to me. I was called in for an interview, along with several of my colleagues who also applied for the position. A week later, I was called in for a second interview, and I was very optimistic that I would get the job. The man who interviewed me seemed to be very much impressed with my résumé and with my responses during the interview. This made me sure that I was going to get the position.

Two days after the second interview, I got a letter from human resources saying that they were very sorry my application was not successful this time and that I should try again the next time there was an opening. This was the third time I had tried for a higher position in the office and been rejected, although I knew I was better qualified than the people they offered the jobs to. I was becoming very discouraged at this point, because it seemed like I was not progressing where my employment was concerned. I was in a state of stagnancy. I was promised when I first joined the company that I could quickly rise through the ranks if I performed well on my job. I had been working very hard over the years and going above and beyond the scope of my duties, and expected to have had it pay off by now. I was very disappointed at how slowly my career was progressing, and was wondering if it was normal or if there was more to it than met the eye.

Although my applications for managerial positions were not successful, this did not stop my colleagues from being jealous of me. They made jokes when they thought I couldn't hear them, about how ambitious I was without having any substance to back it up. Most of them criticized me for every minor thing I did and tried to undermine every progress I made in the office. They dismissed every suggestion I brought up during our office meetings, and made jeering remarks about everything I said. They made me feel like I was unimportant, and not part of them as a team in the office. Sometimes, going to work in the morning was very hard, and I wished I did not have to go. However, I always ended up going, because I did not want to be fired from my job. I had bills to pay and therefore could not afford to just quit the job without anything else to do. I had no joy within me whatsoever, and I knew I had to do something about my situation.

There was one woman who worked in the same department I was in. I avoided her most of the time because she was a little too religious for my liking. She approached me one day and told me she sensed in her spirit that I was not happy and that I was very much frustrated where my career was concerned. She really got my attention, since what she said was very true and I hadn't spoken a word to her or anybody about it. I decided to be honest with her and told her all the high hopes I had for my career and how it seemed to be going nowhere. She took me to a quiet part of the office and prayed with me.

When we had finished praying, she gave me a number to call a friend of hers who is a prophetic minister. This prophetic minister was Dr. Pauline Walley-Daniels. I told her what my problem was, and she told me that I had a lot of envy and jealousy around me and needed to pray a lot to defuse all the missiles that were sent my way. She gave me a sample prayer that I should base my prayer on. Shortly after my first visit with Dr. Walley-Daniels, I felt better about myself and things started changing in my life for the better. I got a job in management in another financial company, which was more prestigious than the company I had worked in previously. The pay was very good, as well as the benefits and the conditions of work. I also saw a lot of progress in my personal life due to the power of prayer. My life has never been the same since I walked into Dr. Pauline's office and she gave me some directions for my life. I saw things from a different perspective, which made me have a more positive attitude toward life. I have learned to commit everything I do into the hands of God, and this has been a great blessing to me since He always answers my prayers. To God be all the glory."

Summary
As we see in the above testimony, it is important that we progress in our employment endeavors since this is the will of God for our lives. We can make that happen through the power of prayer.

Note Page

Strategic Solution Prayer
for
Progressive Employment with Benefit

The Problem
I need progress and promotion in my job.

The Situation
There is a lack of promotion.
I feel a lack of satisfaction on the job.
I feel a lack of respect and honor on the job.
I am experiencing stagnancy and retrogression.

The Goals
I will be effective and productive at work,
that I may find favor with my employers
(directors, supervisors, colleagues, and clients) and
gain promotion to a higher position.
The Lord will grant me the favor
of Ruth and Boaz on the job.

The Authority of Scripture
Proverbs 27:18, Daniel 6:3–5, Acts 6:3, Romans 12:11,
Colossians 4:1, Psalm 123:1, Psalm 75:6

Acts 6:3
Wherefore, brethren, look ye out among you seven men of honest
report, full of the Holy Ghost and wisdom, whom we may *appoint
over this business.*

Romans 12:11
Not slothful in business; fervent in spirit; serving the Lord; ...

Leviticus 19:13
Thou shalt not defraud thy neighbour, neither rob him: the wages of him that is hired shall not abide with thee all night until the morning.

Colossians 4:1
Masters, *give unto your servants that which is just* and equal; knowing that ye also have a Master in heaven.

Psalm 123:1
A Song of degrees
Unto thee lift I up mine eyes, O thou that dwellest in the heavens. Behold, as the eyes of servants look unto the hand of their masters, and as the eyes of a maiden unto the hand of her mistress; so *our eyes wait upon the Lord our God, until that he have mercy upon us.*

Proverbs 27:18
Whoso keepeth the fig tree shall eat the fruit thereof: so he that waiteth on his master shall be honoured.

Psalm 75:6
For *promotion*_cometh neither from the east, nor from the west, nor from the south. But God is the judge: *he putteth down one, and setteth up another.*

Daniel 6:3
Then this Daniel was preferred above the presidents and princes, because an excellent spirit was in him; and the king thought to set him over the whole realm. Then the presidents and princes sought to find occasion against Daniel concerning the kingdom; but they could find none occasion nor fault; forasmuch as he was faithful, neither was there any error or fault found in him. Then said these men, We shall not find any occasion against this Daniel, except we find it against him concerning the law of his God.

Prayer in Action
(Praise, Worship, and Adoration)
Our Father which art in Heaven,
Hallowed be Your name,
Your name is beautiful,
Your name is Holy,
Your name is righteous,
Your name is precious,
Your name is healing,
Your name is deliverance,
Your name is miracle,
Your name is signs and wonders.
Worship and adoration be unto You.
Praise be unto Your name! Amen!
Lord, I come to You
To present the situation on my job.
Lord, I need You to show me Your mercy
And intervene on my behalf.
Lord, according to Your Word in Proverbs 27:18,
"Whoso keepeth the fig tree shall eat the fruit thereof."
Therefore, it is time for me to prosper on my job.
It is time for me to gain promotion.
Lord, Your Word says in Psalm 123:2 that
"as the eyes of servants look unto the hand of their masters, and as
the eyes of a maiden unto the hand of her mistress;
so our eyes wait upon the Lord our God,
until that he have mercy upon us."
O Lord and my Deliverer,
My eyes wait upon You
Until You have mercy upon me.
O Lord, reward my efforts and
"give unto your servants that which is just,"
Because I have not been slothful in business.
Lord, I have been fervent and effective on the job.
I have put in my best to assist and promote
The interests of my job.
But I am yet to be blessed.

O Lord, look upon my tithe and offering
And rebuke the devourer for my sake.
O Lord, look upon my contributions
And support for the ministry,
And recompense me with fruitfulness,
That I may not lack and wallow in poverty.
O Lord, deliver me from stagnancy and poverty.
Deliver me from shame and disgrace,
That I may not be a beggar,
As I have served You, God, in ministry
And also served in my employment.
O Lord, Your Word says the laborer is worthy of his wages.
O Lord, bless me that I may eat the fruit of my effort,
As I have kept the fig tree and the vineyard.
Stir up the heart of my employers, directors,
Supervisors, and colleagues to encourage me
With favor and honor and promotion.
Stir up their hearts to increase my wages.
Motivate them to respect and honor me.
O Lord, recompense me
According to the work of my hands.
O Lord, Your Word declares in Psalm 75:6–7,
"For promotion cometh neither from the east,
nor from the west, nor from the south.
But God is the judge: he putteth down one,
and setteth up another."
O Lord, have mercy on me and promote me this day,
That I may be progressive in my employment.
O Lord, grant me the double portion of favor that You
Granted unto Ruth and Daniel.
Grant me the spirit of excellence.
I would be preferred above the presidents and princes
So that no fault or accusation will come against me.
O Lord, intervene by Your mercies and loving kindness.
Let no one take my place or position.
Let no one rob me of what is due unto me.
Let mercies prevail and deliver me from evil.
Bless me, Lord, that I may pay my tithe and offering.

Bless me, Lord, that I may support Your work.
Bless me, Lord, that I may fulfill my destiny.
Bless me, Lord, that I may praise Your holy name.
Thank You, Lord, for hearing my petition.
Thank You, Lord, for granting me favor.
In Jesus' name I pray. Amen!

Environmental Protection
In the name of Jesus,
And with the authority in the blood of Jesus,
I cover my *business life and employment* with the blood of Jesus.
I plunge my life into the blood of Jesus Christ, my Redeemer,
And seal my *job and promotion* with the blood of Jesus Christ.
The devil will no longer stand against my *business efforts and position*—
Because of the blood of Jesus
That was shed for me.
The blood of Jesus speaks louder than the blood of Abel.
Therefore my *job and business life* are covered
And sealed in the blood of Jesus
Against satanic defilement and corruption.
I release the blood of Jesus to build a wall of protection
Over my business activities.
In Jesus' name I pray. Amen!

Warfare and Confrontation
In the name of Jesus,
And with the authority in the blood of Jesus,
I command you, Satan, and your cohorts to listen to me.
It is written in Proverbs 27:18,
"Whoso keepeth the fig tree
shall eat the fruit thereof:
so he that waiteth on his master
shall be honoured."
It is also written in Luke 10:7
That a laborer is worthy of his pay;
Therefore, you satanic entities
Shall not rob me of my wages and entitlements—in Jesus' name.
You shall not rob me of my promotion and employment—in Jesus' name.

You shall not rob me of my financial resources—in Jesus' name.
You shall not torment or harass me with shame and disgrace—in
Jesus' name.
I bind the spirit of poverty, demotion, oppression, and suppression
That interferes with progress on my job—in Jesus' name.
In the name of Jesus,
I uproot the trees of evil planted against my progress and promotion
And entitlements from my job.
In the name of Jesus, I cast out the satanic arrows of retardation
and stagnancy
That operate within and around my job.
In the name of Jesus, I cast out the terrors that interfere with my
employment, progressiveness, and prosperity from my life.
In the name of Jesus, I command you evil spirits to be evicted and
evacuated right now.
I am no longer your host and you shall not dwell with me.
I am not your partner, and you shall not operate in my employment.
The blood of Jesus raises a standard against you.
The blood of Jesus builds a wall of demarcation against you.
The fire of the Holy Ghost raises a hedge against you.
Go into the Dead Sea and remain there until your judgment day.
In Jesus' name, I command you to go and come no more.
Amen!

Declaration of Solutions
In the name of Jesus,
I stand on the authority in the Word of God
And upon the power in the blood of Jesus
That says that
"Whoso keepeth the fig tree
shall eat the fruit thereof."
Therefore I declare my blessing this day,
That I shall eat from the fruit of my labor.
I declare and decree that I am worthy of my pay.
Therefore the enemy shall not rob me of my wages.
I call forth progress and promotion
To come to me right now.
I declare and decree that this is my time and season

For progressiveness.
Therefore I call forth my favor and honor
To come unto me right now—in Jesus' name.
In the name of Jesus,
I replace poverty with wealth.
I replace stagnancy with progressiveness.
I replace rejection with favor and acceptance.
I replace redundancy with expansion.
I replace demotion with promotion.
Thank You, Lord, for my blessings and prosperity.
Thank You, Lord, for everything!
Amen!

Motivational Song of Victory

"Lead Me, Lord"
Text: Psalms 5:8, 4:8
Music: Samuel Sebastian Wesley

> Lead me, Lord, lead me in thy righteousness;
> make thy way plain before my face.
>
> [Optional]
> For it is thou, Lord, thou, Lord only,
> that makest me dwell in safety.

Prayer Observations and Experiences

Write down your observations and experiences as you say this prayer.

You may remember your dreams and some past occurrences while you are saying it. You may also receive a revelation. It is important that you make notes for future reference.

Observations

_____

_____

_____

_____

_____

Experiences

_____

_____

_____

_____

_____

Part 5

The Relationship Cycle

Chapter Thirteen

Progressive Relationships

Relationships are part of what encourages the continuous existence of mankind on earth. Without relationships, we humans would be isolated in a manner that would make it possible for insecurity and suspicion to destroy our existence.

Relationships promote friendship, friendship promotes understanding, understanding brings unity, unity brings oneness, oneness promotes love, and love brings peace.

Love and peace promote interactions that encourage growth towards a marital relationship. The institution of marriage encourages the growth of the human race, which also leads to sharing and development of communities.

Relationships enable humans to dwell together in a community without fear of enmity.

It is important that we develop our human relationships at all levels, in order to experience progressiveness in our environment and daily endeavors.

There are different kinds of relationships. It is important to open up our relationships to growth and fruitfulness.

A fruitful relationship brings multiplication and abundance of sharing, and partnership in all facets of our human existence.

Everybody needs love and wants to be loved. There are different types of environmental and personal love that we can share, to promote and improve our relationships around the world. Some of the environmental love that we have to learn to share includes brotherly love, friendly love, social love, community love, marital love, and organizational love, all of which are needed in our lives and environment.

Where there is relationship, we can share love with passion and affection comfortably, without fear.

Note Page

Strategic Solution Prayer
for
Progressive Relationships

The Problem
I need progress in my general interactions and relationships.

The Situation
I need trustworthy relationships with friends.
I need sincere relationships with colleagues and partners at work.
I need respectful and honorable relationships with neighbors at home.
I need God-fearing relationships around parents and family members.

The Goals
I will be successful in all my relationships,
that I may find favor with people everywhere I go (Ephesians 1:6).
People will pay attention to me and vice versa (Proverbs 27:10).
I will be respected and honored, in my going out and my coming in.
I will be a blessing to the people I interact with in my daily endeavors.

The Authority of Scripture
Ephesians 4:32, Proverbs 27:10, John 6:70, Philippians 2:13, Hebrews 12:14, 1 Thessalonians 5:15, Ephesians 6:5, Isaiah 53:3, Proverbs 31:18, Ephesians 1:6

Ephesians 4:32
And be ye kind one to another, tenderhearted, forgiving one another, even as God for Christ's sake hath forgiven you.

Proverbs 27:10
Thine own friend, and thy father's friend, forsake not; neither go into thy brother's house in the day of thy calamity: for better is a neighbour that is near than a brother far off.

John 6:70
Jesus answered them, Have not I chosen you twelve, and one of you is a devil? He spake of Judas Iscariot the son of Simon: for he it was that should betray him, being one of the twelve.

Philippians 2:13
For it is God which worketh in you both to will and to do of his good pleasure.

Hebrews 12:14
Follow peace with all men, and holiness, without which no man shall see the Lord: Looking diligently lest any man fail of the grace of God; lest any root of bitterness springing up trouble you, and thereby many be defiled; ...

1 Thessalonians 5:15
See that none render evil for evil unto any man; but ever follow that which is good, both among yourselves, and to all men.

Ephesians 6:5
Servants, be obedient to them that are your masters according
to the flesh, with fear and trembling, in singleness of your heart,
as unto Christ; Not with eyeservice, as menpleasers; but as the
servants of Christ, doing the will of God from the heart.

Isaiah 53:3
He is despised and rejected of men; a man of sorrows, and
acquainted with grief: and we hid as it were our faces from him;
he was despised, and we esteemed him not.

Proverbs 31:18
She perceiveth that her merchandise is good: *her candle goeth not
out by night.*

Ephesians 1:6
To the praise of the glory of his grace, wherein *he hath made us
accepted in the beloved.*

Prayer in Action
(Praise, Worship, and Adoration)
O Lord, my God,
Jehovah God, the Almighty One,
You are the friend among friends,
The friend of the friendless.
You are the one who related to Your servant Moses
And spoke with him
As a friend to a friend.
O Lord, appoint for me
God-fearing people to be my friends—
Associates, colleagues, and neighbors.
Father, You are aware that
I have been despised and rejected
Just as You were despised and rejected.
Lord, my heart is grieved with sorrow

From lies, deception, and accusation.
Hear my cry, O Lord,
And deliver me from the pangs of death
And the sorrows of hell.
Deliver me from those who seek my life
Among friends, colleagues, associates,
Family members, and neighbors.
Lord, deliver me from loneliness
And set my spirit free from rejection and depression.
Father Lord, I ask that Your fear
Arrest each member of my family,
That our relationship will be based
On the fruit of the Spirit,
And that You will surround me with Your presence,
That I would be loved and accepted
As you have made us accepted in Christ Jesus.
Thank you, Lord,
For granting my petition.
In Jesus' name I pray. Amen!

Environmental Protection

In the name of Jesus,
And with the authority in the blood of Jesus,
I cover my *relationships cycle* with the blood of Jesus.
I plunge my *relationships* into the blood of Jesus Christ, my Redeemer,
And seal my *relationships cycle* with the blood of Jesus Christ.
The devil will no longer stand against my *relationships*
with friends, colleagues, family members, and friends—
Because of the blood of Jesus
That was shed for me.
The blood of Jesus speaks louder than the blood of Abel.
Therefore my *relationships cycle* is covered and sealed
In the blood of Jesus
Against satanic interference,
Defilement, and corruption.
The enemy shall no longer have access

Into my relationships—in Jesus' name.
The enemy shall no longer harass
And terrorize my relationships—in Jesus' name.
I release the blood of Jesus Christ to build
A hedge of protection
Around my relationships cycle.
I command the fire of the Holy Ghost
To surround my
Relationships cycle.
In Jesus' name I pray.
Amen!

Warfare and Confrontation
In the name of Jesus,
And with the authority in the blood of Jesus,
Satan, listen to me:
You and your evil entities
Shall not interfere with my relationships,
Because it is written in Ephesians 4:32,
"And be ye kind one to another,
tenderhearted, forgiving one another,
even as God for Christ's sake hath forgiven you."
Therefore I bind any spirit that manipulates the heart of
The people connected to me—in the name of Jesus.
I bind the spirit of unforgiveness
And cast it out of my relationships—in the name of Jesus.
In the name of Jesus, I uproot any satanic power
That causes a person to fall from the grace of God.
In the name of Jesus, I bind and uproot the root of bitterness
Springing up to cause trouble in my relationship cycle.
In the name of Jesus, I bind and uproot any spirit that defiles
My relationship cycle.
In the name of Jesus I cast out the spirit of deception
That hinders sincerity of heart
But promotes eye-service and men-pleasers.
In the name of Jesus, I uproot and cast out

The spirit that renders evil for evil.
In the name of Jesus, I uproot and cast out
Any spirit that hinders me from pleasing God.
In the name of Jesus, and with the authority in the blood of Jesus,
I cast out the spirit that destroys relationships
And I command you to go to the Dead Sea.
You shall no longer interfere with me.
The blood of Jesus builds a boundary between you and me.
The fire of the Holy Ghost raises a wall against you, Satan.
You shall not see me again and I shall not invite you.
Go to the Dead Sea and remain there until your judgment day.
In Jesus' name I pray. Amen!

Declaration of Solutions
In the name of Jesus,
And with the authority in the blood of Jesus,
It is written in Ephesians 4:32,
"And be ye kind one to another,
Tenderhearted, forgiving one another,
even as God for Christ's sake hath forgiven you."
Therefore, I stand on the authority of scriptures
To declare that I shall be kind and tenderhearted to people,
And everyone shall be kind and tenderhearted to me.
In the name of Jesus, it is written,
Forgive us our trespasses as we forgive them that trespass against us.
Therefore I shall not harbor unforgiveness,
And unforgiveness shall not find a room in my heart,
But I shall forgive those who offend me,
And I shall also receive forgiveness from my offenders.
In the name of Jesus, I declare
That I shall not fall short of the grace of God.
The root of bitterness shall not spring up to cause trouble in me
Or in my relationships cycle.
The root of hatred shall not defile me and my relationships.
I declare that there shall be no contamination
Between my colleagues and me at work—in Jesus' name.

I declare that there shall be no confusion or accusation
Between my friends and me—in Jesus' name.
I declare that there shall be no insecurity and suspicion
Between my family members and me—in Jesus' name.
I declare that there shall be no rejection and depression
Between neighbors and myself—in Jesus' name.
In the name of Jesus, I declare unity and understanding around
my relationships.
In the name of Jesus, I declare peace and tranquility around my
relationships.
In the name of Jesus, I declare love and joy around my relationships.
Thank You, Lord, for blessing my relationships.
Amen!

Motivational Song of Victory

"What a Friend We Have in Jesus"
Words: Joseph M. Scriven, 1855
Music: "Erie," Charles C. Converse, 1868

What a Friend we have in Jesus,
All our sins and griefs to bear!
What a privilege to carry
Everything to God in prayer!
O what peace we often forfeit,
O what needless pain we bear,
All because we do not carry
Everything to God in prayer.

Have we trials and temptations?
Is there trouble anywhere?
We should never be discouraged;
Take it to the Lord in prayer.
Can we find a friend so faithful
Who will all our sorrows share?
Jesus knows our every weakness;
Take it to the Lord in prayer.

Are we weak and heavy laden,
Cumbered with a load of care?
Precious Savior, still our refuge,
Take it to the Lord in prayer.

Do your friends despise, forsake you?
Take it to the Lord in prayer!
In His arms He'll take and shield you;
You will find a solace there.

Blessed Savior, Thou hast promised
Thou wilt all our burdens bear.
May we ever, Lord, be bringing
All to Thee in earnest prayer.
Soon in glory bright unclouded
There will be no need for prayer.
Rapture, praise and endless worship
Will be our sweet portion there.

Prayer Observations and Experiences

Write down your observations and experiences as you say this prayer.

You may remember your dreams and some past occurrences while you are saying it. You may also receive a revelation. It is important that you make notes for future reference.

Observations

_____

_____

_____

_____

_____

Experiences

_____

_____

_____

_____

_____

Prayer Observations and Experiences

Chapter Fourteen

Progressive Dating Relationships

Friendship
Dating is a type of relationship that usually leads to marriage. It is wise to develop a friendly relationship with the person one intends to marry. Where there is friendship, there is likely to be a mutual understanding that could help the development of respect for each other.

An opportunity for friendship allows for the growth of friendly love that could develop into a romantic love along the way. In the process of developing a friendly love, one could end up dating a close friend for marriage. A close friend could end up being a best friend, or a friendly relationship could progress into a marital relationship, with good understanding of each other.

It is better to marry your best friend than to dwell with a stranger whom you do not know. A stranger with strange behavior may be a destroyer of life, a pedophile, a rapist, or a criminal.

Dating
Dating is when a man is observing and interacting with a lady with the intention of marrying her. A date may be successful if there is a high level of compatibility and understanding. Dating may not

be successful if one of the parties is not pleased with some of the things that will be discovered down the line.

Also, dating may not be successful because there are too many people in the picture. Sometimes, your dating is not successful because you are encountering some destiny switchers and twisters along the line.

It is important to note that dating is not yet a proposal of marriage. Do not assume you are married to a man until he has proposed to you. Boaz observed Ruth from a distance before drawing her closer to his camp for detailed observations. Ruth 2:8 and 11 reveals thus:

Ruth 2:8

Then said Boaz unto Ruth, Hearest thou not, my daughter? Go not to glean in another field, neither go from hence, but abide here fast by my maidens.

Ruth 2:11

And Boaz answered and said unto her, It hath fully been shewed me, all that thou hast done unto thy mother in law since the death of thine husband: and how thou hast left thy father and thy mother, and the land of thy nativity, and art come unto a people which thou knewest not heretofore.

Examine your situation before you say this prayer.

Note Page

_____

_____

_____

_____

_____

_____

_____

_____

_____

_____

_____

_____

_____

_____

_____

_____

_____

_____

Strategic Solution Prayer
for
Successful Dating Relationships

The Problem
I need progress in my *dating relationship*
with [fill in the name of the brother or sister].

The Situation
I am in too many dating relationships without proposals for marriage.
I have too many suitors without any specific decisions.
The suitors fizzle out after a while.
Friends often snatch my suitors from me.
Family members often reject suitors who approach me.

The Goals
I will have an effective relationship.
I may find favor with the person the Lord has ordained for me.
The Lord will grant me the favor of Ruth and Boaz in my dating.

The Authority of Scripture
Genesis 2:18, Ruth 2:13–16

Genesis 2:18
And the Lord God said, It is not good that the man should be
alone; I will make him an help meet for him.

Ruth 2:13–16

Then she said, Let me find favour in thy sight, my lord; for that thou hast comforted me, and for that thou hast spoken friendly unto thine handmaid, though I be not like unto one of thine handmaidens. And Boaz said unto her, At mealtime come thou hither, and eat of the bread, and dip thy morsel in the vinegar. And she sat beside the reapers: and he reached her parched corn, and she did eat, and was sufficed, and left.
And when she was risen up to glean, Boaz commanded his young men, saying, Let her glean even among the sheaves, and reproach her not: And let fall also some of the handfuls of purpose for her, and leave them, that she may glean them, and rebuke her not.

Prayer in Action
(Praise, Worship, and Adoration)
Jehovah God, our heavenly Father,
You are the rock of ages,
You are the Ancient of Days,
You are Jehovah Adir—the strong one,
You are Jehovah Adon Olam—the master of the world.
Blessed are You, O Lord,
Blessed is the work of Your hands.
You created mankind
And You said it is not good for a man to be alone,
So You made them male and female.
O Lord, although You formed the man out of the ground,
You took the woman out of the man's rib,
And You made the woman
The bone of his bone and the flesh of his flesh
That the two might be one
So that the man would not be alone.
Father, as in the beginning, Your word
Declared that it is not good
For a man to be alone.
O Lord, look upon me and take away loneliness from me.
O Lord, deliver me from singlehood
And make me a partner for life,

That I may raise a family unto You.
O Lord, give me a home and a family
Where the Word of God
Will be the center of my joy,
That no man will mess around with my destiny.
O Lord, grant me the favor of Ruth and Boaz,
That my Boaz (spouse) will find me on the gleaning field
And extend a hand of love to me,
That I may be married.
For it is my heart's desire to be married this day.
O Lord, bless me with a marriage
Where there is no sorrow of heart and rejection,
But a home where there is abundance of love and celebration.
Thank You, Lord, for with You all things are possible.
With You there is fullness of joy.
Thank You, Lord, for taking away loneliness
And granting my heart's desire for marriage. Amen!

Environmental Protection
In the name of Jesus,
And with the authority in the blood of Jesus,
I cover *my desire to marry* with the blood of Jesus.
I plunge *my marriage desire* into the blood of Jesus Christ, my Redeemer,
And seal *my marriage desire* with the blood of Jesus Christ.
The devil will no longer stand against my *desire for marriage*—
Because of the blood of Jesus
That was shed for me.
The blood of Jesus speaks louder than the blood of Abel.
Therefore my *desire for marriage* is covered
And sealed in the blood of Jesus
Against satanic defilement and corruption. Amen!

Warfare and Confrontation
In the name of Jesus,
And with the authority in the blood of Jesus,
I stand on the Word of God
To declare my desire for marriage.
It is written in Genesis 2:18,

"And the Lord God said,
It is not good that the man should be alone;
I will make him an help meet for him."
Therefore I shall not be alone—in the name of Jesus.
Satan, listen to me:
You and your cohorts shall not hinder me
From finding a suitor for marriage.
You and your satanic entities shall not hinder
The advancement of my relationship—in Jesus' name.
I shall not be invited to deceptive dating,
And I shall not yield to unfruitful relationship.
In the name of Jesus, I bind and uproot
Any evil spirit that hinders marital relationship.
In the name of Jesus, I bind and uproot
Any demonic power that contaminates relationship.
In the name of Jesus, I uproot and cast out
Any curse planted against my ability to marry.
In the name of Jesus, I uproot and cast out
Any curse that has been uttered or written
Against my marriage.
In the name of Jesus, I command the curse of singleness
To go out of my body, soul, and spirit.
In the name of Jesus, I command the curse of the unmarried state
To go out of my character, behavior, and attitude.
The blood of Jesus sets me free from the curse of loneliness.
The blood of Jesus releases me from the curse of loneliness.
I release the blood of Jesus to destroy the root of the tree of
loneliness in my life.
The blood of Jesus builds a wall of demarcation between me and
the spirit of loneliness.
The fire of the Holy Ghost builds a hedge of protection
around me.
The spirit of loneliness and unmarried state shall not come close to me.
They shall not see me again—because of the blood of Jesus.
Thank You, Lord, for the great deliverance from unmarried life.
In Jesus' name I pray. Amen!

Declaration of Solutions

In the name of Jesus Christ, my Lord and Savior,
And with the authority in the blood of Jesus that was shed for me,
I stand on the Word of God to call forth my marriage in Jesus' name.
I declare that I shall be found suitable for marriage,
As Ruth the Moabitess was found favorable
By Boaz—in the name of Jesus.
As the word of God declares in Ruth 2:13–16,
"Let me find favour in thy sight, my lord;
For that thou hast comforted me,
And for that thou hast spoken friendly
Unto thine handmaid,
Though I be not like unto one of thine handmaidens.
And Boaz said unto her,
At mealtime come thou hither,
And eat of the bread,
And dip thy morsel in the vinegar."
In the name of Jesus, I declare and decree
That my predestined spouse
Shall invite me for dinner.
In the name of Jesus, I declare and decree
That the Lord shall grant me favor
That my predestined spouse
Will share his or her dining table with me
As Boaz invited Ruth and shared his dinner with her.
For it is written,
"And she sat beside the reapers:
And he reached her parched corn,
And she did eat, and was sufficed, and left."
In the name of Jesus, I declare and decree
That my predestined spouse
Will speak for me and will stand up for me
In every matter that concerns me.
For it is written,
"And when she was risen up to glean,
Boaz commanded his young men, saying,
Let her glean even among the sheaves,

And reproach her not:
And let fall also some of the handfuls
Of purpose for her, and leave them,
That she may glean them, and rebuke her not."
In the name of Jesus, I declare
That so shall it be
That my spouse will make provisions for me
And bless me with the inheritance of the righteous,
That I shall not lack or beg for bread—
Because the favor of the Lord is upon me.
In the name of Jesus, I declare and decree:
Let my marriage come forth right now.
Let my spouse come forth right now—in Jesus' name.
Let the blessing of marriage come to me right now—in Jesus' name.
Let the joy of marriage come to me right now—in Jesus' name.
Let the peace of marriage come to me right now—in Jesus' name.
Let the unity of marriage come to me right now—in Jesus' name.
In the name of Jesus, I declare and decree that
Instead of loneliness, I receive my spouse.
Instead of rejection, I receive acceptance—in Jesus' name.
Instead of depression, I receive celebration—in Jesus' name.
Instead of sadness, I receive joy—in Jesus' name.
The Lord created and blessed marriage.
Therefore I receive the full blessing of marriage
And a happy home in Jesus' name.
Amen!

Dr. Pauline Walley-Daniels

Motivational Song of Victory

"Teach Me Thy Way, O Lord"
Words: Benjamin M. Ramsey, 1919
Music: "Camacha," Benjamin M. Ramsey

Teach me Thy way, O Lord, teach me Thy way!
Thy guiding grace afford, teach me Thy way!
Help me to walk aright, more by faith, less by sight;
Lead me with heav'nly light, teach me Thy way!

When I am sad at heart, teach me Thy way!
When earthly joys depart, teach me Thy way!
In hours of loneliness, in times of dire distress,
In failure or success, teach me Thy way!

When doubts and fears arise, teach me Thy way!
When storms o'erspread the skies, teach me Thy way!
Shine through the cloud and rain, through sorrow, toil and pain;
Make Thou my pathway plain, teach me Thy way!

Long as my life shall last, teach me Thy way!
Where'er my lot be cast, teach me Thy way!
Until the race is run, until the journey's done,
Until the crown is won, teach me Thy way!

Prayer Observations and Experiences

Write down your observations and experiences as you say this prayer.

You may remember your dreams and some past occurrences while you are saying it. You may also receive a revelation. It is important that you make notes for future reference.

Observations

_____

_____

_____

_____

_____

Experiences

_____

_____

_____

_____

_____

Chapter Fifteen

Progressive Courtship Relationships

Courtship begins when dating has been successful. Dating is successful when the man finds the woman to be suitable to be his life partner for a marriage relationship, and then proposes to her.

Courtship is also successful when a woman feels secure and confident that there is passion and affection that stimulates progressive love. A woman feels more secure in a relationship where there is understanding, and provision that could start and establish a progressive family.

As soon as the lady accepts the proposal, the relationship moves from dating to courtship. During courtship, both parties start to interact on a serious note in preparation for marriage. However, the success of a courtship depends on how each person manages his or her temperament and behavior to foster the relationship.

Please examine the kind of relationship you are in, and the situation surrounding it, before you say this prayer. If there is no proposal, then there is no engagement. If there is no engagement, then there is no courtship.

If there is courtship, then you need to pray that your relationship will progress and materialize into a good marriage relationship.

Progressive Courtship Relationship

It is the desire of God that every man should marry and have a partner for life. He even said in the book of Genesis that it is not good for man to be alone. It is also important for man to procreate, because it is God's desire for us to be fruitful and multiply to fill the earth. It is therefore imperative for man to marry in order to be able to have children in a Christian way.

Before one gets married, one has to go through a period of courtship. Courtship must be successful to lead to marriage. However, there are times when courtship is not so successful because of natural and spiritual reasons. The following testimony, which is a direct narration by the subject, is an example of how spiritual forces can affect the progress of courtship. The names have been changed to protect the identity of the individuals involved.

Samina's Story

My name is Samina, and I am happy to share my testimony to show how loving God is, and His desire to set us free from every limitation the devil tries to place on us. I have been having problems in my relationships with the opposite sex for as long as I can remember. Anytime I'm in a relationship with someone, it starts out great, and we end up loving each other deeply. We date for a while, and then the man proposes to me and the relationship moves into the courtship stage. I can barely hide my excitement during this time, whilst I'm busy preparing for the wedding. Somehow, during the course of the courtship, I sense the man pulling away from me for no apparent reason. The relationship that started out with so much passion and excitement suddenly turns cold.

This happened to me on two different occasions. I was heartbroken and embarrassed, and couldn't face my friends and family. I was convinced there was something wrong with me and that I wasn't good enough to be anybody's wife. That left me with extreme low self-esteem. I was also beginning to believe a curse had been placed on me, to prevent me from getting married. I did not really believe much in curses at that time, but there was no logical explanation for what was going on. I therefore turned to God in prayer, to help me and deliver me from this curse, and also to bring someone new into my life. I was hurting and was very lonely and needed to feel loved in order to believe that there was nothing really wrong with me.

About a year and a half after praying to God to bring the man that He had prepared for me to marry, Joshua came into my life. I couldn't have been happier. He proposed to me not long after we started dating, and I accepted his proposal. He said he had been praying for a life partner, and as soon as he set his eyes on me, he knew I was the one for him. I was very happy to hear that from him, and also to know that I had been given a third chance at marriage. We made plans to get married right away because we both decided it felt like the right thing to do.

Two weeks after setting the date for our wedding, I felt Joshua pulling away from me, just like my other two fiancés had done. I couldn't believe this was happening again. I knew I had to do something to put an end to this cycle. I was tired of all the heartache, and I also loved Joshua so much, I just couldn't bear the thought of losing him. I therefore decided to seek help. I did not know whom to turn to. I prayed to God to help me. I felt a peace in my heart after I had prayed, and I knew that God was in control.

A few days after I had prayed, I felt the desire to go for a walk one evening. I walked a long distance from my home, and that turned out to be a very good thing. I passed by a church known as the Overcomers' House Prophetic-Deliverance Church. As I stood staring at the church building, I sensed in my spirit that this was a place where I could find help for all the problems I had been facing concerning my marriage, or the lack thereof. I took down the phone number, and I called the following day. That turned out to be the best phone call I had ever made. I made an appointment with Dr. Pauline, and she took me through some counseling sessions. When I was done with the counseling, she took me through some deliverance ministrations and uprooted every curse that had been placed upon me. I am now free from whatever was holding me back.

My relationship with Joshua improved greatly, and he was eager for us to get married immediately. We did get married, and it was very beautiful and emotional, considering what I had been through. We have been happily married for five years now, and have been blessed with two wonderful children.

My loving advice to anyone who is reading this story is that if you feel things are not going well in your life, seek help from someone who is knowledgeable in spiritual things, and all will be well with you.

Note Page

_____

_____

_____

_____

_____

_____

_____

_____

_____

_____

_____

_____

_____

_____

_____

_____

Strategic Solution Prayer for Successful Courtship That Will Grow into Marriage

The Problem
I need progress in my courtship affairs.

The Situation
I have had many proposals and disappointments.
I have suffered from stagnancy in courtship relationships.
Courtship has tarried for more than a year
and nothing is happening.

The Goals
My courtship relationship will be effective and productive.
I may find favor with my suitor.
The Lord will grant me the favor of Ruth and Boaz in my
relationship.
My courtship will advance to marriage.

The Authority of Scripture
Genesis 2:18 and 21–24; 1 Corinthians 7:1-2

Genesis 2:18
And the Lord God said, It is not good that the man should be
alone; I will make him an help meet for him.

Genesis 2:21–24

And the Lord God caused a deep sleep to fall upon Adam, and he slept: and he took one of his ribs, and closed up the flesh instead thereof; And the rib, which the Lord God had taken from man, made he a woman, and brought her unto the man. And Adam said, This is now bone of my bones, and flesh of my flesh: she shall be called Woman, because she was taken out of Man. Therefore shall a man leave his father and his mother, and shall cleave unto his wife: and they shall be one flesh.

I Corinthians 7:1-2

Now concerning the things whereof ye wrote unto me: *It is* good for a man not to touch a woman. Nevertheless, *to avoid* fornication, let every man have his own wife, and let every woman have her own husband.

Prayer in Action
(Praise, Worship, and Adoration)
Praise to the King of Glory,
Praise to the Lord of Hosts,
Praise to Jehovah God,
The King of Kings and the Lord of Lords.
Worship and adoration be unto the Everlasting Father.
He is the Alpha and Omega,
He is the beginning and the end,
He is the all in all,
He is the great "I Am that I Am."
Blessed be the name of the Lord.
He is our guard and guide.
He is our instructor and director.
Hallelujah to the Prince of Glory! Amen!

Invite the Presence of the Lord
Father, I commit into Your hands
My need and desire for marriage.
Lord, I have had several courtship relationships
But have yet to have one transform into marriage.
Lord, I ask that You look upon my affliction
Of singleness and loneliness

Dr. Pauline Walley-Daniels

And deliver me from the pangs of Sheol
That have prevented my relationship
From progressing into marriage.
O Lord, set me free from rejection.
Deliver me from the curse of barrenness.
Deliver me from the reproach of singleness.
For your word declares in Genesis 2:18
That it is not good for a man to be alone;
Therefore it is not good for me to be alone.
O Lord, it is Your Word
And I stand on the authority of the written Word
To remind You of Your commandment
That authorizes a person not to be alone.
O Lord, watch over Your Word and perform it,
That there shall be a performance of your written Word.
Jehovah Jireh, the Great Provider,
Look upon me and bless me
With the bone of my bone and the flesh of my flesh.
O Lord and my Maker, Jehovah Boreh,
You know the person You have created for my compatibility.
You know the person You sent to this world for me.
You know the person with whom I will serve You.
You know the person with whom I will worship you.
O Lord, my God,
You know the person with whom I will be fruitful.
You know the person with whom I will be fulfilled.
Like an angel, release him/her unto me this day.
Like a dove, send him/her to me this day.
Like a sweet fragrance, let me smell him/her.
Like myrrh, let me preserve him/her.
Like a salt, let me taste his/her affection.
Like honey, let him/her please me.
O Lord, connect me to the love of my life.
Jehovah Jireh, bring us together by Your hands.
Thank you, Lord,
That I will no longer wander in and out of courtship,
For you have settled me according to my prayers
And granted the desires of my heart according to Your Word.
Thank you, Lord. Amen!

Environmental Protection
In the name of Jesus,
And with the authority in the blood of Jesus,
I cover my *courtship life* with the blood of Jesus.
I plunge my *courtship life* into the blood of Jesus Christ, my Redeemer,
And seal my *courtship relationship* with the blood of Jesus Christ.
The devil will no longer stand against my *courtship relationship,*
Because of the blood of Jesus
That was shed for me.
The blood of Jesus speaks louder than the blood of Abel.
Therefore my *courtship* is covered and sealed in the blood of Jesus
Against satanic defilement and corruption. Amen!

Warfare and Confrontation
In the name of Jesus,
With the authority in the blood of Jesus,
I come against satanic activities that prohibit marriage.
For it is written in Genesis 2:18,
"And the Lord God said,
It is not good that the man should be alone;
I will make him an help meet for him."
Therefore, powers and principalities of darkness
Shall not hinder me from marriage in the name of Jesus.
The workers of iniquity shall not repel suitors
From me—in Jesus' name.
I shall not be alone in the name of Jesus.
In the name of Jesus, I bind and uproot
The spirit of loneliness and rejection
That obstructs courtship relationship,
And I command my suitor to come forth—in the name of Jesus.
It is written in Genesis 2:21–24,
"And the Lord God caused a deep sleep to fall upon Adam,
and he slept: and he took one of his ribs,
and closed up the flesh instead thereof;
And the rib, which the Lord God had taken from man,
made he a woman, and brought her unto the man.
And Adam said, This is now bone of my bones,

and flesh of my flesh: she shall be called Woman,
because she was taken out of Man.
Therefore shall a man leave his father and his mother,
and shall cleave unto his wife: and they shall be one flesh."
Satan, listen: this is the Word of the Lord.
Therefore you shall not hinder me from marriage.
You and your cohorts shall not steal or switch my courtship.
In the name of Jesus, I bind and uproot any satanic arrows
Sent against my courtship relationship.
In the name of Jesus, I uproot and cast out any spirit of rejection
Hovering around my courtship relationship.
In the name of Jesus, I uproot and cast out any spirit of confusion
And accusations pestering my courtship relationship.
I release the fire of the Holy Ghost to consume
Any evil spirit interfering with me—in the name of Jesus.
I release the fire of the Holy Ghost against the worker of iniquity
That disturbs my marriage—in Jesus' name.
In the name of Jesus, let the blood of Jesus
Erase the handwriting of curses written
Against my courtship and proposed marriage.
In the name of Jesus, let the blood of Jesus
Wash away the tree of curses planted against my courtship relationship.
In the name of Jesus, let the fire of the Holy Ghost
Consume the root of evil planted against my courtship.
In the name of Jesus, let the fire of the Holy Ghost
Consume the missile of loneliness and rejection
Sent against my courtship relationship.
In the name of Jesus, I evict and evacuate
The spirit of loneliness from my life.
In the name of Jesus, I evict and evacuate
The spirit of rejection and accusations from my life.
In the name of Jesus, you shall not harass me again
And you shall not follow me around.
In the name of Jesus, you shall not visit me or hang around me.
In the name of Jesus, you shall not drive away my suitor.
In the name of Jesus, you shall not repel my suitor with deception.
The blood of Jesus protects me from you, evil spirit.
The blood of Jesus destroys the counsel and activities

Of witches and wizards sent against my progress for marriage.
The blood of Jesus raises a wall of boundary between you and me.
The fire of the Holy Ghost builds a hedge of protection around me.
In the name of Jesus Christ my deliverer, I pray. Amen!

Declaration of Solutions
In the name of Jesus,
And with the authority in the blood of Jesus,
I stand on the Word of God
To declare the institution of marriage
Into my life as it is written in Genesis 2:18,
"And the Lord God said,
It is not good that the man should be alone;
I will make him an help meet for him."
According to the Word of the Lord,
It is not good for me to be alone.
Therefore, I call forth my marriage into being.
I shall not be alone—in the name of Jesus.
I shall not be rejected from marriage—in the name of Jesus.
I shall not be repelled from marriage—in the name of Jesus.
My courtship shall be fruitful—in the name of Jesus.
It is written in Genesis 2:21–24,
"And the Lord God caused a deep sleep to fall upon Adam,
And he slept: and he took one of his ribs,
And closed up the flesh instead thereof;
And the rib, which the Lord God had taken from man,
Made he a woman, and brought her unto the man.
And Adam said, This is now bone of my bones,
And flesh of my flesh: she shall be called Woman,
Because she was taken out of Man.
Therefore shall a man leave his father and his mother,
And shall cleave unto his wife: and they shall be one flesh."
I declare the promises of God concerning me
Shall not fail—in the name of Jesus.
I declare the word that the Lord has spoken
And written concerning me shall prosper.
Therefore, I plant the word of the Lord into my life.
I plant the promises of God into my soul,

Into my heart, into my mind, into my character
And into every facet of my relationship.
My suitor shall find me
And I shall be married.
My spouse shall find me
And I shall be loved and accepted.
My spouse shall find me
And I shall be honored and respected.
As Boaz found Ruth with honor and respect,
So shall I be received with passion and affection—in Jesus' name.
As Ruth inherited a blessing of the promise of Abraham,
So shall I be blessed with the promise
Of my destiny—in Jesus' name.
This day I declare my marital blessings.
It is time for love and acceptance—in Jesus' name.
Now is the time for progressiveness
In my courtship relationship—in Jesus' name.
It is time for my courtship to turn into marriage—in Jesus' name.
No more delay or denial—in Jesus' name,
No more rejection and fault finding or
Accusations—in Jesus' name.
I claim my marriage right now—in Jesus' name.
I declare my victory right now—in Jesus' name.
God has blessed me and no one can curse me—in Jesus' name.
I declare that there shall be no enchantment
Against my courtship and progressiveness—in Jesus' name.
Thank You, Lord, for setting me free from delay and denial.
Thank You, Lord, for releasing me from loneliness and rejection.
Thank You for covering me with love and acceptance.
Thank You, Lord, for blessing me with a happy home.
Blessed be the name of the Lord,
For his love and mercies endure forever.
Amen!

Motivational Song of Victory

"Leaning on the Everlasting Arms"
Words: Elisha A. Hoffman, 1887
Music: Anthony J. Showalter

What a fellowship, what a joy divine,
Leaning on the everlasting arms;
What a blessedness, what a peace is mine,
Leaning on the everlasting arms.

Chorus
Leaning, leaning,
Safe and secure from all alarms;
Leaning, leaning,
I am leaning on the everlasting arms

O how to walk in this pilgrim way,
Leaning on the everlasting arms;
O how bright the path grows from day to day,
Leaning on the everlasting arms.

Chorus

What have I to dread, what have I to fear
Leaning on the everlasting arms;
I have blessed peace with my Lord so near,
Leaning on the everlasting arms.

Prayer Observations and Experiences

Write down your observations and experiences as you say this prayer.

You may remember your dreams and some past occurrences while you are saying it. You may also receive a revelation. It is important that you make notes for future reference.

Observations

_____

_____

_____

_____

_____

Experiences

_____

_____

_____

_____

_____

Chapter Sixteen

Progressive Marital Relationships

The desire for marriage is a thirst for love. Love is the glue that holds a man and a woman together for life till they are parted by death. Seeking a life partner is a desire for a love environment, where destiny is fulfilled. Love is a heart desire that can be satisfied only by marriage:

- A desire for one's flesh to be glued to a bone forever.
- A desire that can never be separated by any situation or circumstance.
- A desire to be loved with passion and affection without interruption.
- A desire to be cared for with knowledge and understanding.
- A desire to settle in a home that produces fruitful generations.
- A desire for a home of peace and joy.

In the beginning, when Jehovah God created humankind, He declared that it is not good for a man to be alone. Immediately, the Lord God opened the rib of the man and made a woman to provide a life partner for the man, so that man would not be alone but would have a companion for a lifetime relationship.

In view of that, marriage is the first and one of the greatest institutions that the Almighty God established, with the creation of humankind. It is important that marriage be respected and honored as a divine institution, and not as a man-made thing that can be disregarded or destroyed.

Marriage is beautiful, and he who finds a wife discovers a good partner more precious than gold. Likewise, a woman who finds a husband has found the heart to which she belongs.

Hence, both the man and woman represent the bone of each other's bone and the flesh of each other's flesh and the two become one—united in heart, body, soul, and spirit.

The Joy of Marriage
The sound of marriage tickles everyone's heart and ignites joy for these reasons:

- Marriage is the greatest destination in destiny.
- Marriage is the fulfillment of life.
- Marriage provides a lifetime satisfaction.
- Marriage is precious.
- Marriage is beautiful.
- Marriage is the root of love.
- Marriage provides satisfaction for love.
- Marriage is the hornet for passion and affection.
- Marriage is the source of reproduction of life.
- Marriage produces the branches of destiny.
- Marriage is the fulfillment and satisfaction of destiny.

Family Interference
The Lord God Almighty established marriage as an institution where people can come together to build family relationships with joy and

peace, but unfortunately, many marital relationships are faced with interference from family members that can be detrimental to their success. The following testimony is an example of how interference from a family member can lead to the breaking up of a family. The woman's name has been changed to protect her privacy.

Sonja's Story

Sonja is an orphan who grew up without knowing who her parents were. She had no siblings, and did not know any of her parents' relatives. She grew up in foster homes where she did not feel loved and therefore could not forge a relationship with any of her foster parents.

Shortly after graduating from college, Sonja met the man of her dreams and they got married after courting for a very brief period.

About a year and a half into the marriage, Sonja got pregnant with their first child. The couple was happy, and they eagerly looked forward to welcoming their child into the world. When the delivery date got closer, Sonja became fretful and anxious about the fact that she did not have anyone to help her with the baby. She therefore discussed the matter with her husband, and they both decided that since she did not have any living relatives, they would bring her husband's mother from abroad to come and live with them so she could help with the baby. Her mother-in-law was happy to be of assistance and made arrangements and came over right away.

When Sonja's mother-in-law came to the States, she was really impressed with the life that her son had created for himself and his family. She was especially impressed with their house, which happened to be the sole property of Sonja, her daughter-in-law. The relationship between mother-in-law and daughter-in-law was cordial from the beginning.

About a month into the mother-in-law's stay, tension started arising between her and Sonja. The mother-in-law, whom we shall call Auntie Bettina, started taking over the house, literally. She accused Sonja of not taking good care of her son. She refused to eat any of the food that Sonja cooked and insisted on preparing her own meals. To make matters worse, she always made it a point to cook her own meals at the very time that Sonja was in the kitchen preparing meals for the family.

In a desperate attempt to salvage whatever relationship was left between her and her mother-in-law, Sonja suggested that Auntie Bettina move into the apartment in the basement. Auntie Bettina interpreted this suggestion to mean that Sonja was throwing her out of the house. She therefore did not bother to hide her hostility toward her daughter-in-law any longer. At this point, Auntie Bettina insisted that her son have dinner with her every night and not eat the food his wife cooked because hers was more nutritious and tasted better than his wife's.

Eventually, Auntie Bettina was able to destroy her son's marriage and actually demanded that Sonja moved out of the house that she had bought with her money. Unfortunately, Auntie Bettina's agenda failed, because the property belonged to Sonja and not her son. She was not successful in her attempt to get the house from Sonja. Rather, Auntie Bettina had to move out of the house with her son, which led to a separation in the marriage.

Interference Caused by Greed

The following story is a true account of how greed can interfere with the success of a marriage. I have changed the woman's name to protect her privacy.

Ionia: I counseled a lady over the phone whom I will refer to as Ionia. She is a very successful businesswoman who owned several properties in a metropolitan city. Although she was very rich, she said she felt empty because she had no one to share her life and riches with. Eventually, God made a way for her, and she met and married a man whom she thought loved her very much.

As soon as her husband discovered that she was very wealthy and owned properties, his attitude toward her changed. Instead of focusing on building the marital relationship, he was interested in how he could best manipulate his wife into transferring the properties to his name. He said since he was the head of the house, it was only proper that all the property be in his name. When Ionia refused to transfer her properties to her husband's name, he withheld his love from her and refused to be a loving husband toward her.

Friendship Interference

Ms. Richardson: It is really sad how some men value their friends more than their marriages. A woman I once counseled in my office came to me crying and complaining about how her husband did not respect her or value their marriage. She complained about how he put the interest of his friends before her own.

Ms. Richardson complained bitterly to me about how she did not feel loved by her husband. He was always inviting friends into their home and expecting her to cook for them and wait on them irrespective of the fact that she had two young children who needed her attention and care. Most of the time, these friends showed up without any prior notice from her husband, and when she complained about it, he told her she was lazy and inhospitable.

The last straw for Ms. Richardson was when her husband left her sitting at the doctor's office for more than two hours after one of her children had an appointment. When she asked why he was so late, he answered off-handedly that one of his friends needed a ride to go somewhere and that was why it had taken him so long to get back to her. He did not even bother to offer an apology for his behavior. This made her felt very worthless and unappreciated by her husband.

What Marriage Isn't
- Marriage is not a soccer field for kicking a spouse like a ball.
- Marriage is not a boxing ring for punching a spouse.
- Marriage is not a wrestling ring for battering a spouse.
- A marital home is not a war zone for abusive behavior.
- A marital home is not a lion's den for assaulting a spouse.
- A spouse is not supposed to be an enemy.
- A spouse is not supposed to be violent.
- A spouse is not supposed to behave like a beast.

Marital aspiration comes with conscious effort. Therefore,

- Aspire to make your marital home like heaven on earth.
- Make a conscious effort to make your home a haven of satisfaction.
- Make a conscious effort to make your home a sanctuary of love.

Note Page

Dr. Pauline Walley-Daniels

Strategic Solution Prayer
for
Progressive Marital Relationship

The Problem
I need progress and promotion in my marriage.

The Situation
Decisions are unconcluded and ineffective.
There are unnecessary arguments.
There are unnecessary principles.
There are too many rules and regulations.
I feel like I'm in a master-servant relationship.
I am experiencing spiritual interferences with nightmares and horrors.
I am experiencing material interferences with finances and properties.
I am experiencing emotional interferences with infidelity and cheating.
I am experiencing physical interferences with health and barrenness.

The Goals
I will have a progressive marriage.
The Lord will knit our hearts together as husband and wife.
I will find favor with my spouse and in-laws.
The Lord will grant me the favor
of Ruth and Boaz on my marital activities.
I will experience joy and peace in my marriage.
There will be true love, passion, and affection in my marital life.
Fear of the unknown will be over.
My marriage will be a treasure of destiny fulfillment.
That my spouse will respect and honor me.

The Authority of Scripture
Genesis 2:22–25, Ruth 1:15–18, Ruth 4:13-15, Matthew 19:4–6

Genesis 2:22–25
And the rib, which the Lord God had taken from man, made he a woman, and brought her unto the man. And Adam said, This is now bone of my bones, and flesh of my flesh: she shall be called Woman, because she was taken out of Man. Therefore shall a man leave his father and his mother, and shall cleave unto his wife: and they shall be one flesh. And they were both naked, the man and his wife, and were not ashamed.

Ruth 1:15-18
And she said, Behold, thy sister in law is gone back unto her people, and unto her gods: return thou after thy sister in law. And Ruth said, Intreat me not to leave thee, *or* to return from following after thee: for whither thou goest, I will go; and where thou lodgest, I will lodge: thy people *shall be* my people, and thy God my God: Where thou diest, will I die, and there will I be buried: the LORD do so to me, and more also, *if ought* but death part thee and me. When she saw that she was stedfastly minded to go with her, then she left speaking unto her.

Ruth 4:13–15
So Boaz took Ruth, and she was his wife: and when he went in unto her, the Lord gave her conception, and she bare a son. And the women said unto Naomi, Blessed be the Lord, which hath not left thee this day without a kinsman, that his name may be famous in Israel. And he shall be unto thee a restorer of thy life, and a nourisher of thine old age: for thy daughter in law, which loveth thee, which is better to thee than seven sons, hath born him.

Matthew 19:4-6
And he answered and said unto them, Have ye not read, that he
which made them at the beginning made them male and female,
And said, For this cause shall a man leave father and mother,
and shall cleave to his wife: and they twain shall be one flesh?
Wherefore they are no more twain, but one flesh. What therefore
God hath joined together, let not man put asunder.

Prayer in Action
(Praise, Worship, and Adoration)
O Lord God of Abraham, Isaac, and Jacob,
The Lord God of Israel,
The Creator of heaven and earth,
The God who instituted marriage on earth,
You are worthy to be praised.
Jehovah God, the God who commanded that
It is not good for man to be alone,
Your Word is yea and amen.
Your Word is authority and life.
You deserve the glory and honor.
O Lord God, blessed are you among the gods.
You are highly exalted far above the heavens.
Glory, honor, praise, and adoration be unto you. Amen!
O Lord, my Father,
I come to present my marriage to you this moment.
O Lord, my marriage is clouded with
Unfulfilled and ineffective decisions.
O Lord, deliver my marriage from lack
Of communication and understanding,
And inject the expression of affection and passion
Into our marriage life.
O Lord, set my marriage free from arguments
And outbursts of wrath,
And inject wisdom and peace into our home.
O Lord, deliver my marriage from unnecessary principles—
Too many rules and regulations.
O Lord, deliver my marriage from

A master-servant relationship,
And inject true love and joy into our hearts
So that we would experience the joy of salvation in our home.
O Lord, remember Your Word that commands,
And deliver me from the evil of divorce and separation.
Dear Lord, You promised to watch over Your Word to perform it.
Therefore perform a miracle of love and understanding
In my marriage and home.
O Lord, remember that it is your purpose for a man and woman to leave
their father and mother and dwell together in marriage as one flesh.
Therefore intervene in this matter and
Stir up love and unity in my marriage.
O Lord, set my spirit free that I may praise Your name.
O Lord, let all bondage go and let deliverance flow.
O Lord, give us a Christian home where we would be able to
worship You
In spirit and in truth.
Lord, Your Word says in Matthew 19:5–6,
"… For this cause shall a man leave father and mother,
And shall cleave to his wife: and they twain shall be one flesh?
Wherefore they are no more twain, but one flesh.
What therefore God hath joined together,
Let not man put asunder."
Therefore, I ask that you would
Give us a home where we would celebrate and praise your name.
O Lord, turn the stony hearts in our marriage into hearts of flesh.
O Lord, deliver our marriage from insecurity and suspicion.
O Lord, deliver my spouse from dishonesty and unfaithfulness.
O Lord, inject your spirit of purity and holiness into our marriage.
O Lord, arrest us with the fear of God.
O Lord, let the spirit of righteousness arrest our souls.
Jehovah God, let the spirit of humility
And simplicity take over our total beings,
That we may know you and serve You with one accord.
Thank You, Lord, for salvaging our marriage from evil.
In Jesus' name I pray. Amen!

Environmental Protection
In the name of Jesus,
And with the authority in the blood of Jesus,
I cover *my marriage life* with the blood of Jesus.
I plunge *my marriage* into the blood of Jesus Christ, my Redeemer.
And seal *my marriage life* with the blood of Jesus Christ.
The devil will no longer stand against the prosperity of *my marriage*
Because of the blood of Jesus
That was shed for me.
The blood of Jesus speaks louder than the blood of Abel.
Therefore *my marriage life* is covered and sealed in the blood of Jesus
Against satanic defilement and corruption.
I release the blood of Jesus as a protection
Against shame, disgrace,
And embarrassment in my marriage;
In the name of Jesus, I release
The fire of the Holy Ghost as a hedge
Of protection over my marriage. Amen!

Warfare and Confrontation
In the name of Jesus,
And with the authority in the blood of Jesus,
Satan, listen to me.
You and your powers and principalities of darkness
Shall not interfere with my marriage—
Because of the Word of the Lord.
I stand on the authority of the Word of God
That instituted marriage from the beginning.
According to Genesis 2:22–24,
"And the rib, which the Lord God had taken from man,
Made he a woman, and brought her unto the man.
And Adam said, This is now bone of my bones,
And flesh of my flesh: she shall be called Woman,
Because she was taken out of Man.
Therefore shall a man leave his father and his mother,
And shall cleave unto his wife:
And they shall be one flesh.

And they were both naked,
The man and his wife,
And were not ashamed."
Therefore you shall not interfere with my marriage.
Satan, you shall not separate me from my spouse.
Witches and wizards shall not switch the blessing of my marriage.
Workers of iniquity shall not exchange my spouse with evil.
The Word of God declares,
"What therefore God hath joined together,
let not man put asunder."
Therefore, powers and principalities of darkness,
Or rulers and agents of darkness
Shall not pull my marriage apart.
In the name of Jesus, I bind and uproot the element
Of divorce and separation sent against my marriage.
With the authority in the blood of Jesus,
I bind and uproot handwritings of satanic verses
Published against the prosperity of my marriage.
In the name of Jesus, I uproot and cast out
Any negative pronouncement uttered against the
Love and unity of my marital home.
In the name of Jesus, I uproot and cast out
The arrow of evil sent against my marriage.
In the name of Jesus, I uproot and cast out
The arrows of dishonesty and unfaithfulness
That disrupt and interfere with my marriage.
In the name of Jesus, I uproot and cast out
The missile of confusion and insecurity
Planted against my marriage.
In the name of Jesus, I uproot and cast out
The missiles of anger and accusations
Planted against my marriage.
In the name of Jesus, I uproot and cast out
The trees of ungodliness planted against
The survival of my marriage.
In the name of Jesus, let the fire of the Holy Ghost
Destroy the arrows of evil sent against my marriage.
In the name of Jesus, let the blood of Jesus nullify

The arrows and missiles sent against my marriage.
In the name of Jesus, let the blood of Jesus raise
A standard against the works and workers of iniquity.
In the name of Jesus, let the blood of Jesus raise
A fortress around my marriage.
In the name of Jesus, let the fire of the Holy Ghost
Build a hedge of fire around my marriage and home.
Satan, your powers and principalities of darkness,
Rulers, and cohorts shall not come
Close to my marriage or home.
You shall not touch or interfere with or disrupt my family.
You shall no longer have access to my marriage—
Because of the blood of Jesus
And the fire of the Holy Ghost.
In the name of Jesus, I evict and evacuate
Your activities from my marriage and home.
In Jesus' name I pray. Amen!

Declaration of Solutions
In the name of Jesus,
And with the authority in the blood of Jesus,
I declare and decree that the counsel of
The Most High God over my marriage shall be
As it is written in Genesis 2:22–24,
"And the rib,
which the Lord God had taken from man,
made he a woman,
and brought her unto the man.
And Adam said,
This is now bone of my bones,
and flesh of my flesh:
she shall be called Woman,
because she was taken out of Man.
Therefore shall a man leave
his father and his mother,
and shall cleave unto his wife:
and they shall be one flesh.
And they were both naked,

the man and his wife,
and were not ashamed."
In the name of Jesus,
I declare and decree unity and love in my marriage.
I declare and decree that my spouse shall not know
Any other person but me.
In the name of Jesus, the desire of my spouse
Shall be unto me.
It is written in Matthew 19:6,
"What therefore God hath joined together,
let not man put asunder."
Therefore, nothing shall interfere with my marriage.
In the name of Jesus I declare and decree that
No satanic activity shall pull us apart.
My marriage is covered in the blood of Jesus.
My marriage is protected in the name of Jesus.
My spouse shall love me in the name of Jesus.
My spouse shall respect and honor me in the name of Jesus.
My spouse shall be faithful and honest to me in the name of Jesus.
My spouse shall not see another person
Besides me—in the name of Jesus.
I shall be loved and accepted—in the name of Jesus.
There shall be no anger and accusations
Around my marriage—in the name of Jesus.
There shall be love and affection
In my marriage—in the name of Jesus.
Thank You, Lord, for blessing my marriage.
Thank You for uniting our hearts together in love.
Thank You for granting my heart's desire—in the name of Jesus.
Thank you, Jehovah Jireh.
Amen!

Motivational Song of Victory

"O Perfect Love"
Words: Dorothy F. Gurney, 1883
Music: "Perfect Love," Joseph Barnby, 1890

O perfect Love, all human thought transcending,
Lowly we kneel in prayer before Thy throne,
That theirs may be the love which knows no ending,
Whom Thou forevermore dost join in one.

O perfect Life, be Thou their full assurance,
Of tender charity and steadfast faith,
Of patient hope and quiet, brave endurance,
With childlike trust that fears nor pain nor death.

Grant them the joy which brightens earthly sorrow;
Grant them the peace which calms all earthly strife,
And to life's day the glorious unknown morrow
That dawns upon eternal love and life.

Hear us, O Father, gracious and forgiving,
Through Jesus Christ, Thy coeternal Word,
Who, with the Holy Ghost, by all things living
Now and to endless ages art adored.

Prayer Observations and Experiences

Write down your observations and experiences as you say this prayer.

You may remember your dreams and some past occurrences while you are saying it. You may also receive a revelation. It is important that you make notes for future reference.

Observations

_____

_____

_____

_____

_____

Experiences

_____

_____

_____

_____

_____

Part 6

Realms of Fruitfulness

Chapter Seventeen

Fruitfulness

Fruitfulness means "to be fertile." It is the ability to bear fruit in abundance. It means to be favorable to the growth of fruit. It means to be useful for vegetation.

Fruitfulness also means "to be productive or prolific." It means one's work is profitable. One's effort is yielding positive results. A person's ability is beneficial. Fruitfulness yields benefit. Bearing children is fruitfulness of the womb.

The marriage relationship was originally blessed to be fruitful. Marriage was the first institution that God blessed with fruitfulness and fulfillment. The man was commanded to take a compatible woman for his wife, and they were to work together toward productive and fruitful life endeavors to fulfill their destiny on earth as it is in heaven.

Friendship is supposed to be a fruitful relationship where you are free to share and receive from one another. A friendship should be given the opportunity to flourish and bear fruits that satisfy.

Business is supposed to be fruitful for one to gain profit to sustain one's daily endeavor and provide for the home. Whenever a business fails, a home is affected and the joy of a family relationship is paralyzed. Lack of productivity is a cankerworm that destroys the hope and encouragement of a hardworking person.

Academic education is supposed to be fruitful for one to gain professional wealth to prepare for life. A good academic result opens the door to greater heights of expectation. A fruitful academic effort paves the way for promotion and excellence in one's destiny.

God created us to be fruitful in all that we do. In fact, He said in His Word that we should be fruitful and multiply. Therefore, it is His desire to see us prosper in all that we lay our hands on or set out to do. God also wants us to be able to maintain whatever blessings He gives us without losing them. The only way we can obtain wealth and maintain it is through prayer and committing all that we have to God. The following testimony, as told directly by the individual involved, tells us how important it is for us to pray that God will protect all that He has blessed us with. The woman's name has been changed to protect her privacy.

Ruddy's Story

My name is Ruddy. I went to see Dr. Pauline Walley-Daniels a few years ago because of a problem I was having with children in my marriage. My husband and I had been married for five years when we were blessed with a very handsome baby boy after trying for so long. He was the joy of our lives, and we loved him very much. When my son turned three, I started having strange dreams about him. Most nights, I dreamt that he was very sick and my husband and I had to rush him to the emergency room. Just as the doctor came to examine him and was about to tell us what was wrong with him, I woke up. Anytime I woke up from such a dream, I would find out that my son had a temperature and was not feeling well. I would then have to take my son to the emergency room, just as I saw in the dream. After a series of tests, the doctors could not find anything wrong with my baby. This went on for a while, and my husband and I were at our wits' end. Our sweet little baby boy was suffering so much in his health, and there was nothing the doctors or my husband and I could do to help him. I kept on having the same dream at least once a week, and the cycle of having to take him to the hospital after having the dream continued.

When my son was about eight years old, the frequency of the dreams intensified, and his health kept on failing. There was nobody I knew at that time whom I could confide in or turn to for help. I knew my son needed more than the regular medical attention he was getting. However, I did not know where to turn for such help. One day, when I had the same dream I had been having for years about my son, something about the dream was quite different. This time, the doctor diagnosed what was wrong with my baby. However, I could not remember what it was when I woke up.

Later that afternoon, Junior got very sick and my husband and I had to rush him to the emergency room. The doctor said he had a congenital heart defect that should have been diagnosed several years ago. Somehow, the doctors had failed to do so, and it was now too late to operate and mend the heart. He needed a heart transplant immediately in order to survive. However, since there wasn't one available for him, my baby died. I was really distraught and could not stop crying for a long time.

It was during this time of mourning that I met a friend whom I hadn't seen in a very long time. She told me I needed to be prayed for and that she knew of a good deliverance minister who could help me. It was then that she introduced me to Dr. Pauline Walley-Daniels. She took me through counseling and also prayed for me. I then realized that Junior might still be alive if I had met her earlier for her to pray for us. Within a short time of meeting with Dr. Walley-Daniels, my husband and I received healing for all the hurt and disappointments we had been through. Soon after, I became pregnant and we have since had three children. We realized the power of prayer and how it can change our circumstances in life.

Note Page

_____

_____

_____

_____

_____

_____

_____

_____

_____

_____

_____

_____

_____

_____

_____

_____

_____

Strategic Solution Prayer for Fruitfulness and Increase

The Problem
I need to be fruitful in my biological womb.
I need for my seed to increase with abundance.

The Situation
My marriage has been childless.
I have not been fertile in my spiritual and physical womb.
I have also not been productive and fruitful in my body.

The Goals
I will bear children.
I will be fertile, productive, and fruitful.
I will flourish in my body.

The Authority of Scripture
Genesis 1:28, Psalm 1:3, Psalm 128:1-6, Matthew 19:26

Genesis 1:28
And God blessed them, and God said unto them, Be fruitful,
and multiply, and replenish the earth, and subdue it: and have
dominion over the fish of the sea, and over the fowl of the air, and
over every living thing that moveth upon the earth.

Psalm 1:3
And he shall be like a tree planted by the rivers of water, that bringeth forth his fruit in his season; his leaf also shall not wither; and whatsoever he doeth shall prosper.

Psalm 128:1-6
A Song of degrees
Blessed is every one that feareth the Lord; that walketh in his ways. For thou shalt eat the labour of thine hands: happy shalt thou be, and it shall be well with thee. Thy wife shall be as a fruitful vine by the sides of thine house: thy children like olive plants round about thy table. Behold, that thus shall the man be blessed that feareth the Lord. The Lord shall bless thee out of Zion: and thou shalt see the good of Jerusalem all the days of thy life. Yea, thou shalt see thy children's children, and peace upon Israel.

Matthew 19:26
But Jesus beheld *them,* and said unto them, With men this is impossible; but with God all things are possible.

Prayer in Action
(Praise, Worship, and Adoration)
O Lord, my God,
The great God of wonders,
The great and everlasting Father,
Jehovah Elohim—the God who parted the Red Sea,
Jehovah Jireh—the God who provided manna
For Israel in the wilderness;
Jehovah Shammah, the ever-present God,
You are the one who led Israel
By the pillar of cloud by day
And the pillar of fire by night;
Jehovah Boreh, the Creator of all things,
O Jehovah God, You are the one who spoke
And things came into existence.

O Lord, the power of creation is in Your mouth
And Your utterance goes forth with instant manifestation.
You said, "Let there be light,"
And light came into existence instantly.
You are the God I know and serve.
O Lord, be thou exalted above the heavens.
Jehovah God, be thou glorified in all things.
Jehovah God, You created mankind
In Your own image and likeness
And You commanded them in Genesis 1:28,
"And God blessed them,
and God said unto them,
Be fruitful, and multiply,
and replenish the earth,
and subdue it:
and have dominion over the fish of the sea,
and over the fowl of the air,
and over every living thing that moveth upon the earth."
O Lord, it is time to perform your word
Upon my life;
O Lord, it time to manifest your word in me
As it was in the beginning.
O Lord, You are the covenant-keeping God.
Your word and promise have never failed.
You are the God who opened Sarah's womb
At an old age of ninety years,
And Isaac was born.
You are the God who surprised Elizabeth
At an old age, and John the Baptist was born.
Jehovah Jireh, You are the one who heard
And answered Hannah's cry
And blessed her with Samuel.
You are the one who remembered Rachel,
And she bore Joseph and Benjamin.
O Lord, my God,
You are the only solution to my need.

Although the human doctors have said
It is impossible,
You are the God who makes the impossible
To become possible,
For Your Word declares in Matthew 19:26,
"But Jesus beheld them,
and said unto them,
With men this is impossible;
but with God all things are possible."
Great God of wonders,
I call upon You to have mercy upon me
And open my womb that I may conceive
By Your hand;
Jehovah Jireh, show me Your favor
And visit me as You visited Sarah and Elizabeth.
Jehovah Jireh, You are able to intervene in my case
As You intervened in the case of Hannah.
Great God of Wonders,
Your Word says in Mark 9:23,
"Jesus said unto him,
If thou canst believe,
all things are possible to him that believeth."
Yes, Lord, I believe Your Word.
I believe You can do it.
I believe You would do it for me.
O Lord, You are the one who visited
The Virgin Mary and put a child in her womb
When she had had no contact with a man;
Therefore I believe above all things
That You can do it for me.
O Lord, take the reproach of barrenness
Away from me and bless me with children.
O Lord, cause my womb to be fertilized
That I may have children;
It is Your Word and command
In Psalm 1:1,

"Blessed is the man that walketh not
in the counsel of the ungodly,
nor standeth in the way of sinners,
nor sitteth in the seat of the scornful.
But his delight is in the law of the Lord;
and in his law doth he meditate day and night.
And he shall be like a tree planted by the rivers of water,
that bringeth forth his fruit in his season;
his leaf also shall not wither;
and whatsoever he doeth shall prosper."
O Lord, forgive me if I have wandered away
From Your Word;
Wash me in the blood that You shed for me
On the cross of Calvary,
That I may be worthy to receive
The blessings of fruitfulness in my womb.
O Lord, let me be like a tree
Planted by the rivers of water
That brings forth fruit in season.
Jehovah Jireh, bless me,
That I may prosper in my marriage.
For it is written in
Psalm 128:1,
A Song of degrees,
"Blessed is every one that feareth the Lord;
that walketh in his ways.
For thou shalt eat the labour of thine hands:
happy shalt thou be,
and it shall be well with thee.
Thy wife shall be as a fruitful vine
by the sides of thine house:
thy children like olive plants
round about thy table.
Behold, that thus shall the man be blessed
that feareth the Lord.
The Lord shall bless thee out of Zion:

and thou shalt see the good of Jerusalem
all the days of thy life.
Yea, thou shalt see thy children's children,
and peace upon Israel."
O Lord, hear my cry
And make me a fruitful vine.
O Lord, hear my petition
And bless me with children
Who will be planted like olive trees
Around my table;
Bless me, Lord, and enable me
To see my children's children,
That my children shall praise Your name,
That my children shall worship and honor Your name,
That my children shall be a testimony to Your works,
That my children will serve You from generation to generation.
Thank You, Lord, for hearing my cry.
Thank You, Lord, for granting my petition.
Thank You, Lord, for opening my womb.
Thank You, Lord, for blessing me with children
Who will be planted like olive trees
In the house of the Lord;
To You be all the praise and adoration. Amen!

Environmental Protection
In the name of Jesus,
And with the authority in the blood of Jesus,
I cover *my womb* with the blood of Jesus.
I plunge *my womb* into the blood of Jesus Christ, my Redeemer,
And seal my womb with the blood of Jesus Christ.
The devil will no longer stand against *my fertility to bear children*⸺
Because of the blood of Jesus
That was shed for me.
The blood of Jesus speaks louder than the blood of Abel.
Therefore I release the blood of Jesus
To wash and cleanse *my womb*

From any contamination,
Tumor, or disease—in Jesus' name.
I release the fire of the Holy Ghost
To consume the root of barrenness
From my womb—in the name of Jesus.
I release the blood of Jesus
To seal *my womb*
Against satanic defilement
And corruption—in Jesus' name. Amen!

Warfare and Confrontation
In the name of Jesus,
And with the authority in the blood of Jesus,
I come against you, Satan.
In the name of Jesus,
I come against you and your cohorts.
In the name of Jesus, I come with the blood of Jesus
And the authority that is in the name above all names.
Listen, Satan, it is written in the beginning.
In Genesis 1:28, it says,
"And God blessed them,
and God said unto them,
Be fruitful, and multiply,
and replenish the earth,
and subdue it:
and have dominion over the fish of the sea,
and over the fowl of the air,
and over every living thing that moveth upon the earth."
Therefore the spirit of barrenness shall no longer harass me.
In the name of Jesus, I bind and uproot
The spirit of barrenness out of my womb;
In the name of Jesus, I uproot and cast out
The spirit of barrenness.
Go out of my womb right now—in Jesus' name.
In the name of Jesus,
I bind and uproot you, curse of barrenness,

Pronounced or written against me directly or indirectly.
The blood of Jesus is against you.
Go out of my life—in the name of Jesus.
For it is written in Psalm 128:1,
A Song of degrees,
Blessed is every one that feareth the Lord;
that walketh in his ways.
For thou shalt eat the labour of thine hands:
happy shalt thou be,
and it shall be well with thee.
Thy wife shall be as a fruitful vine
by the sides of thine house:
thy children like olive plants
round about thy table.
Behold, that thus shall the man be blessed
that feareth the Lord.
The Lord shall bless thee out of Zion:
and thou shalt see the good of Jerusalem
all the days of thy life.
Yea, thou shalt see thy children's children,
and peace upon Israel."
Therefore you shall not deprive me
Of my ability to bear children, Devil.
You shall not frustrate my marriage
With infertility, Devil.
You shall not reproach my marriage
With barrenness, Devil.
Go out of my marriage right now—in Jesus' name.
With the authority in the blood of Jesus,
I bind and uproot any diabolical activity
Sent against me in the realm of wickedness.
The blood of Jesus is against you, Devil.
Go out of my life in the name of Jesus.
With the authority in the blood of Jesus,
I uproot and cast out handwriting of ordinances
Printed against my fertility;

The blood of Jesus nullifies your impact in my life.
Go out of my womb right now—in the name of Jesus.
You, spirit of envy and jealousy prying into my marriage,
You shall not succeed—in the name of Jesus.
The blood of Jesus nullifies your evil works.
Go out of my life, Devil.
In the name of Jesus, you shall no longer
Interfere with or harass my womb.
In the name of Jesus, you shall no longer
Terrorize my marriage with childlessness.
The blood of Jesus raises a standard
Against your devilish activities.
Go out of my life right now—in Jesus' name.
In the name of Jesus, I evict
And evacuate you out of my womb.
I shall not be a host to you, Devil,
And you shall not visit me—in Jesus' name.
I shall not entertain you, Devil,
And you shall not hang around me—in Jesus' name.
The blood of Jesus raises a wall of demarcation
Between you and me.
The fire of the Holy Ghost builds
A hedge of protection around my life and womb;
Go to the Dead Sea, Devil,
And remain there until your judgment day.
In Jesus' name I command you. Amen!

Declaration of Solutions
In the name of Jesus,
And with the authority in the blood of Jesus,
I declare and decree that the counsel of the Most High God
Upon my marriage and womb,
That I shall not be barren,
But I shall be fruitful in Jesus' name.
I shall be pregnant and
Bear my own children naturally.

I shall conceive and
There shall be no miscarriage—in Jesus' name.
For it is written in Genesis 1:28,
And God blessed them,
and God said unto them,
Be fruitful, and multiply,
and replenish the earth,
and subdue it:
and have dominion over the fish of the sea,
and over the fowl of the air,
and over every living thing that moveth upon the earth.
Therefore I declare my womb to be fruitful in Jesus' name.
I call forth my womb to conceive right now—in Jesus' name.
There shall be no tumor or disease in my womb—in Jesus' name.
The blood of Jesus release my womb
For productivity—in Jesus' name;
For it is written in
Psalm 128:1,
A Song of degrees,
Blessed is every one that feareth the Lord;
that walketh in his ways.
For thou shalt eat the labour of thine hands:
happy shalt thou be,
and it shall be well with thee.
Thy wife shall be as a fruitful vine
by the sides of thine house:
thy children like olive plants
round about thy table.
Behold, that thus shall the man be blessed
that feareth the Lord.
The Lord shall bless thee out of Zion:
and thou shalt see the good of Jerusalem
all the days of thy life.
Yea, thou shalt see thy children's children,
and peace upon Israel.
Thank You, Lord. Amen!

Motivational Song of Victory

"Bringing in the Sheaves"
Words: Knowles Shaw, 1874. Shaw wrote music for these lyrics, but
George Minor's tune is universally used today.
Music: George A. Minor, 1880

Sowing in the morning, sowing seeds of kindness,
Sowing in the noontide and the dewy eve;
Waiting for the harvest, and the time of reaping,
We shall come rejoicing, bringing in the sheaves.

Refrain

Bringing in the sheaves, bringing in the sheaves,
We shall come rejoicing, bringing in the sheaves,
Bringing in the sheaves, bringing in the sheaves,
We shall come rejoicing, bringing in the sheaves,

Sowing in the sunshine, sowing in the shadows,
Fearing neither clouds nor winter's chilling breeze;
By and by the harvest, and the labor ended,
We shall come rejoicing, bringing in the sheaves.

Refrain

Going forth with weeping, sowing for the Master,

Though the loss sustained our spirit often grieves;
When our weeping's over, He will bid us welcome,
We shall come rejoicing, bringing in the sheaves.

Refrain

Prayer Observations and Experiences

Write down your observations and experiences as you say this prayer.

You may remember your dreams and some past occurrences while you are saying it. You may also receive a revelation. It is important that you make notes for future reference.

Observations

_____

_____

_____

_____

_____

Experiences

_____

_____

_____

_____

Chapter Eighteen

Blessings

Another word for *fruitfulness* is "blessing." A person who is fruitful in marriage or in business can be referred to as being blessed.

Blessings are good omens, which Jehovah God has poured unto the works of His hands as He created them in the beginning. God blessed everything that He made, including the birds of the air, the beasts in the field, and the plants with their herbs.

However, the Almighty God gave His personal ability to humankind as a blessing. Humankind was blessed to have dominion over everything on earth and to subdue it.

The blessings include the authority to have the plants, herbs, animals, birds, and fishes for consumption.

God is merciful and gracious in pouring out His blessings upon mankind. As part of the dominion that God has given to us,

- We are blessed to declare and proclaim blessings upon our lives.
- We are blessed to receive as we give.
- We are blessed to procreate as we marry.
- We are blessed to establish a home and raise a family.
- We are blessed to use our gifts and talents.

- We are blessed to establish businesses and make profits.
- We are blessed to live and to make progress in our life endeavors.

Even if we do not recognize our blessings, God still opens the windows of heaven and pours out His abundance upon us. Some of us have been made distributors of the blessings of God, but we give to others generously, sparingly, or stingily.

Some people don't have much, yet they are great givers and supporters of God's blessings, and some others have been reduced to mere consumers because of mysterious challenges and difficulties. However, there are those who never seek to give or distribute for fear of lack or lack of knowledge; hence they are ridden by poverty.

Blessings are good to desire. Everyone must practice the act of blessing directly and indirectly to experience unique blessing and abundance.

What is the act of blessing?

- To speak positive things to somebody and about others.
- To encourage somebody.
- To share pleasantries with a smile.
- To celebrate one another.
- To give to the needy.
- To share good things with others.
- To share our joy and peace with others.
- To acknowledge the efforts of others even if they seem insignificant.
- To admire others even if they appear too simple.
- To say thank you for every little help or assistance.

Note Page

Strategic Solution Prayer
for
Blessings

The Problem
I need the blessing of God.

The Situation
I need the blessing of positive pronouncement and declarations.
I need to experience the signs of blessings.
I need favor that attracts blessings.

The Goals
God will bless me with fruitfulness, increase, and replenishment
in abundance.
I will live in peace and joy.
The Lord will enlarge the boarders of my coast with abundance.

The Authority of Scripture
Genesis 12:1–3, Numbers 23:18–24, 24:5–7, Chronicles 4:9-10

Genesis 12:1
Now the Lord had said unto Abram, Get thee out of thy country,
and from thy kindred, and from thy father's house, unto a land
that I will shew thee: And I will make of thee a great nation, and
I will bless thee, and make thy name great; and thou shalt be a
blessing: And I will bless them that bless thee, and curse him that
curseth thee: and in thee shall all families of the earth be blessed.

Numbers 23:19–23

God is not a man, that he should lie; neither the son of man, that he should repent: hath he said, and shall he not do it? or hath he spoken, and shall he not make it good? Behold, I have received commandment to bless: and he hath blessed; and I cannot reverse it. He hath not beheld iniquity in Jacob, neither hath he seen perverseness in Israel: the Lord his God is with him, and the shout of a king is among them. God brought them out of Egypt; he hath as it were the strength of an unicorn. Surely there is no enchantment against Jacob, neither is there any divination against Israel: according to this time it shall be said of Jacob and of Israel, What hath God wrought!

Numbers 24:5

How goodly are thy tents, O Jacob, and thy tabernacles, O Israel! As the valleys are they spread forth, as gardens by the river's side, as the trees of lign aloes which the Lord hath planted, and as cedar trees beside the waters. He shall pour the water out of his buckets, and his seed shall be in many waters, and his king shall be higher than Agag, and his kingdom shall be exalted.

I Chronicles 4:9-10

And Jabez was more honourable than his brethren: and his mother called his name Jabez, saying, Because I bare him with sorrow. And Jabez called on the God of Israel, saying, Oh that thou wouldest bless me indeed, and enlarge my coast, and that thine hand might be with me, and that thou wouldest keep *me* from evil, that it may not grieve me! And God granted him that which he requested.

Prayer in Action
(Praise, Worship, and Adoration)
Father of Heaven,
King of Glory and Lord of all,
The great God of wonders,
The Ancient of Days and the rock of ages,
Blessed Redeemer and living word,
You are the God of blessings and the righteous one.
Hallowed be Your name, O Lord, my God.
Thank You for who You are. Amen!

Prayer of Petition

Father, I have come to request blessings of You.
As you blessed Abraham, Isaac, and Jacob,
So bless me with the blessing of heaven and earth.
According to Genesis 12:2,
"And I will make of thee a great nation,
and I will bless thee,
and make thy name great;
and thou shalt be a blessing."
O Lord, bless me
According to Your riches in glory,
That I may be a choice vine of blessings
In Your kingdom.
According to Numbers 23:20,
"Behold, I have received commandment to bless:
and he hath blessed; and I cannot reverse it."
O, Lord, Your Word also says in Numbers 24:5–7,
"How goodly are thy tents, O Jacob,
and thy tabernacles, O Israel!
As the valleys are they spread forth,
as gardens by the river's side,
as the trees of lign aloes which the Lord hath planted,
and as cedar trees beside the waters.
He shall pour the water out of his buckets,
and his seed shall be in many waters,
and his king shall be higher than Agag,
and his kingdom shall be exalted."
O Lord, bless me like a garden planted
By the river side that my seed may be in many waters;
O Lord, pour out Your blessing according to Psalm 1:1–3:
"Blessed is the man that walketh not
in the counsel of the ungodly,
nor standeth in the way of sinners,
nor sitteth in the seat of the scornful.
But his delight is in the law of the Lord;

and in his law doth he meditate day and night.
And he shall be like a tree planted by the rivers of water,
that bringeth forth his fruit in his season;
his leaf also shall not wither;
and whatsoever he doeth shall prosper."
O Lord, make me a fruitful vine.
Plant me like an olive tree by the rivers of living water,
That I may bear fruit in season and out of season;
Thank You, Lord, for granting my heart's desire. Amen!

Declaration of Blessing
In the name of Jesus,
It is written in Genesis 1:28,
"And the Lord God said,
Be fruitful and multiply
And replenish the earth and subdue it."
Therefore I declare the
Word of the Lord into my soul, spirit, and body;
I declare that the fruit of my body shall multiply—in Jesus' name.
Let there be fruitfulness in my body—in Jesus' name.
Let there be multiplication of my fruit—in Jesus' name.
Let there be replenishment in my body—in Jesus' name. Amen!
In the name of Jesus, and with the authority in the blood of Jesus,
I declare that no contrary spirit shall hang around me.
In the name of Jesus, I release my blessings of fruitfulness.
In the name of Jesus, I release attraction for blessings upon my life.
In the name of Jesus, I release the favor of blessings upon my
daily endeavors.
In the name of Jesus, I release the favor of blessings
Upon my going out and my coming in,
Upon my employment,
Upon my relationship cycles,
Upon my marriage, and
Upon my educational endeavors.
In the name of Jesus, I release the blood of Jesus
To cover my blessings;

In the name of Jesus, the enemy shall not touch my blessings.
The arm of destruction shall not touch my blessings—in Jesus' name.
The terror of depression shall not harass my blessings—in Jesus' name.
I uproot any tree of oppression planted against my blessings—in
Jesus' name.
The blood of Jesus raises a standard
Against any stray missiles wandering around my blessings.
Thank You, Lord, for releasing divine blessings over my life.
Amen!

Motivational Song of Victory

"Count Your Blessings"
Words: Johnson Oatman Jr.
Music: Edwin O. Excell (Chicago: 1897)

> When upon life's billows you are tempest tossed,
> When you are discouraged, thinking all is lost,
> Count your many blessings, name them one by one,
> And it will surprise you what the Lord hath done.

Refrain

> Count your blessings, name them one by one,
> Count your blessings, see what God hath done!

> Count your blessings, name them one by one,
> And it will surprise you what the Lord hath done.

> Are you ever burdened with a load of care?
> Does the cross seem heavy you are called to bear?
> Count your many blessings, every doubt will fly,
> And you will keep singing as the days go by.

Refrain

When you look at others with their lands and gold,
Think that Christ has promised you His wealth untold;
Count your many blessings. Wealth can never buy
Your reward in heaven, nor your home on high.

Refrain

So, amid the conflict whether great or small,
Do not be disheartened, God is over all;
Count your many blessings, angels will attend,
Help and comfort give you to your journey's end.

Prayer Observations and Experiences

Write down your observations and experiences as you say this prayer.

You may remember your dreams and some past occurrences while you are saying it. You may also receive a revelation. It is important that you make notes for future reference.

Observations

_____

_____

_____

_____

_____

Experiences

_____

_____

_____

_____

_____

Part 7

Realms of Warfare

Chapter Nineteen

Uprooting Curses

A curse is the opposite of blessing. When we open our mouth to speak, our utterance is either a positive pronouncement that encourages or a negative word that hurts.

When we exhibit a behavior, our action demonstrates an act of blessing or depicts a negative attitude. A curse is a culture of evil and an act of the enemy. A curse is an act of destruction and element of perdition.

At no time should anyone entertain an act of a curse. People who are under the influence of a curse suffer pain and distress. Placing a curse causes people to struggle for everything in life, even for a cup of water or coffee.

A curse is an evil that hunts a person to death.

- A curse can make a professional person live in penury.
- A curse may cause a professional person to live in debt and never enjoy the blessing of his or her work.
- A curse may cause a person to suffer accidental challenges frequently.
- A curse may cause a person to live in stagnation in the midst of opportunity.

- A curse may cause a person to suffer physical ailment without just cause.
- A curse may be a repercussion of an offense committed by an unknown family member.
- A curse may be a pronouncement made out of envy and jealousy.
- A curse may be a declaration made out of ignorance.
- A curse may be a conspiracy against a person's progressive life.

All acts of placing curses must be uprooted and destroyed in order to:
- uproot and destroy from your environment the element that generates curses;
- uproot and cast away from your environment the behavior that depicts the act of placing curses;
- disassociate from the elements that encourage evil;
- sop cursing the people around you so that you will not be contaminated by your own actions; and
- reverse every curse that you have ever uttered or planted against yourself, and start to replace them with blessings.

It is also very important to make it a habit to reverse every curse that might have been uttered against you. More often than not, people do not curse us to our face or in our hearing. It is therefore imperative that we reverse every unknown curse in order to avoid satanic manifestations against our lives and environment.

If we realize that things are not working in our lives the way they should be, or we find ourselves going around in circles, we should consider the possibility of being under some form of curse and have it uprooted. We should not tolerate a state of stagnancy.

It is very important that we progress in all that we do, including our employment endeavors. Stagnancy should not be a part of us as Christians. Just as the Holy Spirit is progressive, so must every aspect of our lives be advanced from time to time if the Holy Spirit is within us, and if we are really living according to the will of God. The state of advancement should include our employment status and everything that concerns us.

Prayer is the key to making sure we advance in the way that God wants us to advance. It also serves as ammunition against every satanic missile thrown our way to prevent us from fulfilling our destiny. The following testimony is a direct account of someone I counseled, and it tells how lack of prayer can open us up to the attacks of the enemy and thereby be kicked out of our destiny. His name has been changed to protect his privacy.

Haniel's Story

My name is Haniel. I was a medical doctor by profession and had been practicing medicine for the past twelve years. Working as a physician was my passion, and I had wanted to do it ever since I could remember. The day I graduated from medical school was one of the happiest and most fulfilling days of my life, as well as that of my parents. They were so proud of me, and that made me very happy. They did not have much education themselves; neither did most of the members of their families. Most of their family members either dropped out of high school or did not even bother going to high school at all. In fact, I was the first doctor in the family.

Not too long ago, about three years to be precise, a friend of mine invited me to a party. Initially, I did not want to go. This was because anytime I went out with this particular friend, he tried to set me up with a woman. This was a problem, because although the women he tried to set me up with were good women, I believe they were just not my type. Yet he couldn't understand why I wasn't interested in these women. He kept insisting that it was high time I married and settled down since I wasn't getting any younger.

Nicolas (that's the name of my friend) finally managed to talk me into going to the party with him. This was a very upscale party with lots of intellectuals and influential people. I was actually enjoying myself when Nicolas approached me with yet another woman. She appeared to be a nice woman, but yet again, not my type. However, I did not turn her down but pretended to like her because my friends had started teasing me and asking lots of questions about whether I was sure of my sexual orientation. They had started asking if it was possible for me to like any woman at all since I had turned down everyone Nico had tried to fix me up with. I therefore decided to go along with it and see how far it would go.

Nandy and I (not her real name) started dating. It did not take long for me to realize we had a lot of differences that could pose a problem in our relationship. It did not take long for that to happen, and I eventually lost interest in the relationship. I started to withdraw from her emotionally and physically, and she started showing a different side of her nature, which was worse than anything I had seen. I told her I could not go on with the relationship, and that was when things really got bad. She cursed me and told me my life would never be the same again, and that nothing I did would ever prosper. I just shrugged it off and thought they were just words and couldn't hurt me. I was really wrong about that.

A month after we broke up, I lost my job as a result of a minor incident that happened at work concerning a patient. This patient accused me of things that were not true. I was brought before the hospital board, and after some questioning, they decided to relieve me of my post and have my medical license revoked. I felt like I was in a very bad dream that I could not wake up from. I lost my house and my car and found myself homeless. I had nobody to turn to. I couldn't go back to my parents. As a matter of fact, I did not have the heart to tell them I had lost my job and my license to practice medicine. I strongly believe I was going through all these misfortunes because of the curse Nandy pronounced on me. I decided I needed help to have the curse broken off me. I therefore got in touch with Dr. Pauline Walley-Daniels through the help of a friend. Things have started to turn around in my life for the better, and I know that by the grace of God, they will continue to do so.

Summary

The above testimony confirms how a curse that is not dealt with the proper way can affect our whole lives and destiny in a negative way.

Note Page

Strategic Solution Prayer Against the Arrows of Curses

The Problem

I need to destroy curses that obstruct my progress and blessing.

The Situation

I need to stop hearing evil pronouncements.
I need to stop the negative declarations made against me.
I need to resist the arrows of anger,
hatred, and bitterness directed toward my blessings and progress,
that the workers of iniquity will not have access to my life,
blessings, and achievements.

The Goal

The curses and evil pronouncements made against me shall not prosper.

Authority of Scripture
Genesis 12:3, Numbers 23:22–23, Isaiah 54:14–17

Genesis 12:3
And I will bless them that bless thee, and curse him that curseth
thee: and in thee shall all families of the earth be blessed.

Numbers 23:22-23
God brought them out of Egypt; he hath as it were the strength of an unicorn. Surely there is no enchantment against Jacob, neither is there any divination against Israel: according to this time it shall be said of Jacob and of Israel, What hath God wrought!

Isaiah 54:14
In righteousness shalt thou be established: thou shalt be far from oppression; for thou shalt not fear: and from terror; for it shall not come near thee. Behold, they shall surely gather together, but not by me: whosoever shall gather together against thee shall fall for thy sake. Behold, I have created the smith that bloweth the coals in the fire, and that bringeth forth an instrument for his work; and I have created the waster to destroy. No weapon that is formed against thee shall prosper; and every tongue that shall rise against thee in judgment thou shalt condemn. This is the heritage of the servants of the Lord, and their righteousness is of me, saith the Lord.

Prayer in Action
(Praise, Worship, and Adoration)
In the name of Jesus,
With the authority in the blood of Jesus,
I stand on the Word of the Lord
To declare the counsel of the
Most High God according to Numbers 23:23,
"Surely there is no enchantment against Jacob,
neither is there any divination against Israel:
according to this time
it shall be said of Jacob and of Israel,
What hath God wrought!"
Therefore, I stand on the Word of God this day,
To declare that there shall be no enchantment
Against me, [fill in your name].
I am a descendant of Abraham by faith.
Therefore there shall be no enchantment
Against me and my family—in Jesus' name.
There shall be no entanglement against my

Employment and promotion—in Jesus' name.
There shall be no enchantment against
My marriage and family—in Jesus' name.
There shall be no enchantment against
My relationship cycles—in Jesus' name.

Declaration of Solutions

In the name of Jesus, and with the authority in the blood of Jesus,
Satan, listen to me: the blood of Jesus Christ that was shed on the
cross of Calvary is a standard against you and your cohorts.
Therefore, I raise a wall of demarcation between you and me.
In the name of Jesus, I declare and decree a signpost against your
operations:
In the name of Jesus, Satan, no stopping.
In the name of Jesus, Satan, no standing.
In the name of Jesus, Satan, no waiting.
In the name of Jesus, Satan, no picking up.
In the name of Jesus, Satan, no stealing.
In the name of Jesus, Satan, no robbery.
In the name of Jesus, Satan, no killing.
In the name of Jesus, Satan, no harassing.
In the name of Jesus, Satan, no terrorizing.
In the name of Jesus, Satan, keep moving to the Dead Sea
And wait there until your judgment day.
The blood of Jesus covers me and my family
Against any arrow of curses sent by day or by night.
Let brimstone fire from heaven consume the arrows of curses,
Sent since the generation of my ancestors.
In the name of Jesus, let the fire of the Holy Ghost build a hedge
of protection
Around me and my family members.
In the name of Jesus, let the fire of the Holy Ghost destroy
The arrows of the curses that afflict my body, soul, and spirit.
In the name of Jesus, I make this decree and declaration. Amen!

Motivational Song of Victory

"Jesus Loves Even Me"
Words and Music by Philip P. Bliss, 1838–1876

I am so glad that our Father in heav'n
Tells of His love in the Book He has giv'n;
Wonderful things in the Bible I see
This is the dearest, that Jesus loves me.

Tho I forget Him and wander away,
Still He doth love me wherever I stray;
Back to His dear loving arms would I flee,
When I remember that Jesus loves me.

O if there's only one song I can sing
When in His beauty I see the great King,
This shall my song in eternity be:
"O what a wonder, that Jesus loves me!"

Jesus loves me, and I know I love Him;
Love brought Him down my poor soul to redeem;
Yes, it was love made Him die on the tree;
Oh, I am certain that Jesus loves me!

If one should ask of me, how can I tell?
Glory to Jesus, I know very well!

God's Holy Spirit with mine doth agree,
Constantly witnessing Jesus loves me.

In this assurance I find sweetest rest,
Trusting in Jesus, I know I am blessed;
Satan, dismayed, from my soul now doth flee,
When I just tell him that Jesus loves me.

Chorus
I am so glad that Jesus loves me,
Jesus loves me, Jesus loves me;
I am so glad that Jesus loves me,
Jesus loves even me.
Jesus loves even me.

Prayer Observations and Experiences

Write down your observations and experiences as you say this prayer.

You may remember your dreams and some past occurrences while you are saying it. You may also receive a revelation. It is important that you make notes for future reference.

Observations

_____

_____

_____

_____

_____

Experiences

_____

_____

_____

_____

_____

Chapter Twenty

Breaking Yokes

A yoke is a burden that the enemy lays upon an individual so that the person is oppressed by situations that may be abnormal. A yoke is also a form of bondage that keeps one in a state of stagnation or retrogression.

A yoke may also be a repercussion of a curse that emanated from one's ancestors or a previous generation. A yoke is an oppressive burden that causes displeasure and discomfort in a person's life.

Sometimes, an enemy may invoke a curse upon a person in a form of a burden, so that one is held in some form of imprisonment for life. Unless the yoke is broken, one may carry a false burden for the rest of one's life.

As mentioned above, the enemy places yokes on humans in the form of stagnancy and retrogression. The following testimony is from a member of my ministry who had such yokes broken off from her life. Her name has been changed to protect her identity and privacy.

Megan's Story
My name is Megan, and I am a member of Overcomers' House Church. My life had been a series of failures until quite recently, when I was ministered to by Dr. Pauline and the yoke that was besetting me was broken, and I have been set free from the powers of darkness.

I am a university graduate and completed my bachelor's degree fifteen years ago. My life was pretty normal in terms of progression, up until the time I finished the university. Anything I tried to do after that seemed to be met with a lot of resistance. The relationship I had been in since my second year at the university failed after a series of problems. I traveled abroad to study for a post-graduate course but had to defer it, although I was nearing completion, for lack of funds. I eventually abandoned it and never went back to finish it.

Every job I had after that did not last for more than a few months. Everything I tried my hand at failed and never came to an expected end. I was the subject of ridicule by some of my friends and family. They had a strong notion that I was unable to keep a job because I was lazy, and they just made snide remarks at me every chance they got.

I had a strong desire to go back to school to study for my master's, but again, circumstances prevented me from doing so. My situation made it impossible for me to obtain a student loan, and I could not afford to pay out of pocket since I did not have any savings due to my frequent unemployment. I therefore ended up doing menial jobs since I couldn't find anything that befitted what I knew I was more qualified to do. I was very disheartened, and my spirit was really crushed, but I knew I could not give up. I just could not allow the enemy to win. I felt within me I was born for more than this kind of mediocre life. I purposed in my heart that I was not going to let this cycle of stagnancy and retrogression get the better of me. I had to be victorious and be who God created me to be.

It was at this time that I decided to go to Dr. Pauline for counseling and deliverance ministration, if there was the need for deliverance. We met for several counseling sessions, and she advised me to sign up for deliverance ministration. I signed up and went through with the deliverance, and my life has never been the same. Every yoke was broken off of me, and I have been free since then. The cycle of stagnancy and retrogression has stopped completely, and I see a lot of progression in my life. Everything I do comes to an expected end, and I no longer have any problem maintaining a job. The power of God is available to us to break any yoke that besets us, and we must tap into that power as often as we need to and it will never fail us.

Note Page

Strategic Solution Prayer
for
Breaking Yokes

Problem
I am bedeviled by the yoke of curses.

Situation
I am going around in circles.
I am unable to make progress in my endeavors.
I am unable to achieve set goals.
I have too many unfinished projects.
I have unfulfilled plans and promises.
I am influenced by procrastination.

Goals
I will break the cycle of stagnancy.
I will overcome procrastination.
I will accomplish set goals.
I will break the yoke of curses.

Authority of Scripture
Numbers 23:23

Surely there is *no enchantment* against Jacob, neither is there any *divination* against Israel: according to this time it shall be said of Jacob and of Israel, What hath God wrought! (Emphasis added.)

Prayer in Action
(Praise, Worship, and Adoration)
Praise be to the Lord God Almighty,
The God of all battles,
Who teaches my hands to make war
Against the enemy of my progress.
Praise be to the Lord God Most Holy,
Jehovah El-Gibbor, who fights my battles.
O Lord, unto You, I submit my life.
Unto You, I present my challenges and difficulty.
O Lord, unto You, I turn over my battles this day,
That You will fight for and defend me
Against the problems that have bedeviled my life.
Jehovah God, take over until my enemies are defeated;
Take over and fight until my enemis perish.
Thank You, Lord,
For You will never leave me or forsake me.
Thank You for agreeing to fight my battles.
In the name of Jesus Christ, our Lord and Savior,
I pray with thanksgiving. Amen!

Environmental Protection
In the name of Jesus,
And with the authority of the blood
That was shed on the cross of Calvary,
Let my life be protected from the arrows of iniquity.
Let my soul be saturated with the blood of Jesus,
Let my life be surrounded by the fire of the Holy Ghost,
Let my family and household be covered under the shadow
Of the Almighty,
Let the blood of Jesus raise a defense for my family
Against all manner of satanic attacks and demonic outrages.
In the name of Jesus Christ, my Lord and Savior. Amen!

Warfare and Confrontation

In the name of Jesus,
And with the authority of the blood
That was shed on the cross of Calvary,
I raise a standard against satanic burdens
That confront me in the daytime and by night,
In the spiritual and physical realms
And in every realm of my existence.
In the name of Jesus, I come against the arms of satanic arrows
That are sent against me
To create false burdens around my environment
And to weigh me down.
In the name of Jesus, I release the blood of Jesus
Against the yoke of depression, suppression, oppression, and frustration.
In the name of Jesus Christ, my Redeemer,
I cancel and dismiss the yoke of satanic assaults and violations
That are listed against me and my family.
In the name of Jesus I uproot the trees of satanic yokes
From my neck and shoulder.
In the name of Jesus I uproot and cast out
The yoke of curses from my head and my chest.
In the name of Jesus I release myself from false burdens
And from the yoke of deception that seems to consume my attention.
In the name of Jesus, I command the fire of the Holy Ghost to destroy
The root of all manner of satanic yokes in my life.
In the name of Jesus, let brimstone fire from above
Consume the root and manifestation of demonic yokes
That interfere with my life.
In the name of Jesus, I release my life and my name,
My home and my family, my job and my finances, and all that
belongs to me
From the yoke of satanic assaults and violations,
And I declare my environment "out of bounds" to the enemy.
I command a total eviction and destruction of handwritings of
ordinances
That permit the enemy to have access to my life.
In the name of Jesus, I command my spiritual and physical doors

To be shut and locked against the enemy.
I withdraw any permit that allows the enemy to gain access to my life.
In the name of Jesus I declare and decree no entry into my life.
In the name of Jesus, the enemy shall no longer gain access
To assault and violate my life.
In the name of Jesus, today is the last time
The enemy will violate my life with satanic yokes of depression,
oppression, suppression, and frustration. Amen!

Declaration of Solution
In the name of Jesus,
With the authority in the blood of Jesus,
I stand on the Word of the Lord
To declare the counsel of the
Most High God, according to Numbers 23:23,
"Surely there is no enchantment against Jacob,
neither is there any divination against Israel:
according to this time
it shall be said of Jacob and of Israel,
What hath God wrought!"
I stand on the Word of God this day
To declare and decree that there shall be no enchantment
Against me, [fill in your name].
I declare and decree that I am a descendant of Abraham by faith.
Therefore there shall be no enchantment
Against me and my family—in Jesus' name.
I declare and decree that there shall be no entanglement
Against my employment and promotion—in Jesus' name.
I declare and decree that there shall be no enchantment
Against my marriage and family—in Jesus' name.
I declare and decree that there shall be no enchantment
Against my relationship cycles—in Jesus' name. Amen!

Motivational Song of Victory

"Victory In Jesus"
Author: Eugene Bartlett
Year Written: 1939

I heard an old, old story,
How a Savior came from glory,
How He gave His life on Calvary
To save a wretch like me;
I heard about His groaning,
Of His precious blood's atoning,
Then I repented of my sins
And won the victory.

Chorus
O victory in Jesus,
My Savior, forever.
He sought me and bought me
With His redeeming blood;
He loved me ere I knew Him
And all my love is due Him,
He plunged me to victory,
Beneath the cleansing flood.

I heard about His healing,
Of His cleansing pow'r revealing.
How He made the lame to walk again

And caused the blind to see;
And then I cried, "Dear Jesus,
Come and heal my broken spirit,"
And somehow Jesus came and bro't
To me the victory.

I heard about a mansion
He has built for me in glory.
And I heard about the streets of gold
Beyond the crystal sea;
About the angels singing,
And the old redemption story,
And some sweet day I'll sing up there
The song of victory.

Prayer Observations and Experiences

Write down your observations and experiences as you say this prayer.

You may remember your dreams and some past occurrences while you are saying it. You may also receive a revelation. It is important that you make notes for future reference.

Observations

_____

_____

_____

_____

_____

Experiences

_____

_____

_____

_____

Chapter Twenty-One

Destroying Demonic Arrows

A demonic arrow is a weapon of satanic warfare. It is an instrument for devising evil against a person. It is ammunition for paralyzing innocent people and causing misfortune, mysterious problems, mishaps, and other forms of evil.

A demonic arrow is also witchcraft power that is wielded against a targeted person.

Demonic arrows are used for the following reasons:
- To inflict sicknesses and diseases
- To cast spells on people or things
- To destroy the life of a person
- To inflict mental confusion
- To cause psychological affliction
- To cast the spirit of death on a person

Demonic arrows are a kind of affliction that the enemy uses to torment people so that they suffer constant pain and unrest in their physical body.

Attacks from demonic arrows include the following:

- Headaches and body pains
- A sensation of crawling or movement in the body
- Loss of limbs and certain members of the physical body
- Dizziness and weakness
- Feeling of depression or death
- Frequent loss of employment
- Frequent loss of financial opportunities
- Frequent accidents
- Feeling of numbness and paralysis in certain parts of the body
- Hatred of spouse or dislike of family members
- Frequent disagreements among family members and friends
- Frequent feelings of rejection and dejection

It is more common than we think it is to find people in our societies who are the targets of demonic arrows being thrown at them from all directions, thereby impeding their progress in life.

The testimony I am about to share with you is about a young lady by the name of Brenda. I have obtained permission from her to use her story to shed more light on this topic.

Brenda's Story

Brenda is a very beautiful young lady who came to see me in my office about a year ago. As soon as she walked into the office, I could tell by her countenance that she was a troubled young woman who had a lot on her mind. Within a few minutes of speaking with her, I realized that she was the target of a lot of demonic arrows. Her complaints ranged from lack of employment to failure in almost everything she put her hand to. She was very discouraged and convinced that she was not destined to be successful in life.

Arrow of Unemployment: One of Brenda's major setbacks in life was her inability to find meaningful employment. Even if she was lucky to find something that enabled her to make a decent livelihood, she couldn't maintain it and lost it in no time. This seemed to be the story of her life. She went through this cycle of problems for several years until one day, she got a job with an organization after crying to God in persistent prayer. She loved her job as well as her colleagues very much, and looked forward to going to work every day. She was very good at what she did, and her boss was very much pleased with her.

Arrow of Sickness: Another way Brenda was targeted by demonic arrows was through her health. Shortly after she started this job, Brenda started having health problems. She was fit and healthy when she was unemployed, but when she started this new job, which she loved, the enemy decided to attack her health to keep her from performing it well.

After going through several medical examinations as a result of her ill health, the radiologist found a lump in her breast that he was very concerned about. A biopsy of the lump came back negative, but the doctors were still concerned and decided to monitor her closely.

Almost six months after the lump was removed, the radiologist found some calcifications on her chest wall during one of her follow-up tests. Also at this time she discovered that one of her aunts had died from a similar ailment. That awareness aroused some level of concern in her mind.

Arrow of Rejection and Dejection: One other demonic arrow that was being hurled in Brenda's direction was the frequent feeling of rejection and dejection. Most of her relationships were not successful. She lost friends as easily as she made them. The story of her romantic relationship was also the same. It was always difficult for her to meet someone she was interested in for dating toward marriage. If she was fortunate enough to find such a person, it did not take long for him to break up the relationship over something trivial.

Deliverance Ministration: I arranged for several counseling sessions with Brenda, and then scheduled her for deliverance ministration. During the ministration, my assistant pastors and I prayed and destroyed all the demonic arrows that were being launched at her.

Today, Brenda is free from all the torments she had to endure as a result of the demonic arrows, and she is gainfully and happily employed. Her health has also improved dramatically, and she is no longer being monitored closely by her doctors. Her relationships have also improved, and she is happily married to the man of her dreams. We give all the glory to God.

Note Page

Strategic Solution Prayer
to
Destroy the Arrows of Evil and Death

Problem
I am overwhelmed by too many problems at the same time.

Situation
I am surrounded by too many problems.
Every direction I turn seems to be under satanic siege.
It's as though I am under physical house arrest.
Everywhere is blocked and I am limited.
I am not able to reach out to anyone or anything.
My ability to reason has almost come to a standstill.

Goals
Someone will rescue me from perishing.
I will receive urgent help and assistance to crush the enemy of my
progress.
The chains will be broken and the prison gates will be opened.
I will be released from the pangs of suicide and the claws of evil.

Authority of Scripture
Psalm 18:1–50

The *sorrows of death* compassed me, and the *floods of ungodly men*
made me afraid.

The *sorrows of hell* compassed me about: the *snares of death*
prevented me.
In my distress I called upon the Lord, and cried unto my God: *he
heard my voice out of his temple, and my cry came before him, even
into his ears* ...

The Lord also *thundered in the heavens, and the Highest gave his
voice; hail stones_and coals of fire.*
Yea, *he sent out his arrows,* and *scattered them*; and he shot out
lightnings, and discomfited them.
Then the channels of waters were seen, and the foundations of the
world were discovered at thy rebuke, O Lord, at the blast of the
breath of thy nostrils.
He sent from above, *he took me, he drew me out of many waters.*
He *delivered me from my strong enemy,* and from them which hated
me: for they were too strong for me.
They *prevented me in the day of my calamity*: but the Lord was my stay.
He brought me forth also into a large place; he delivered me,
because he delighted in me.
The Lord *rewarded me according to my righteousness; according to
the cleanness of my hands hath he recompensed me.*
*For I have kept the ways of the Lord, and have not wickedly departed
from my God...* (Emphasis added.)

Prayer in Action
(Praise, Worship, and Adoration)
Praise God from whom all blessings flow.
Praise Jehovah God Almighty,
Whose power to salvage is beyond human comprehension;
Praise the King of Glory and the Lord of All,
Who delivers and sets one free from the arrows of evil.
Praise the great God of wonders,
Who listens and hears the cry of his children.
His name be praised and uplifted far above all others. Amen!

Environmental Protection
In the name of Jesus,
And with the authority in the blood
That was shed on the cross of Calvary,
Let my life be protected from the arrows of evil
That torment my life every day and night.
Let my soul be saturated with the blood of Jesus
Against the arrows of death that hunt my existence.
Let my life be surrounded by the fire of the Holy Ghost
Against witchcraft and demonic enchantments.
Let my family and household be covered
Under the shadow of the Almighty
Against the arrows that fly by day and the terror by night.
Let the blood of Jesus raise a defense for my family
Against all manner of satanic attacks and demonic outrages.
In the name of Jesus Christ, my Lord and Savior,
Who fights every battle that concerns me. Amen!

Warfare and Confrontation
In the name of Jesus,
And with the authority of the blood
That was shed on the cross of Calvary,
I come against the arrows of evil
That are launched against my existence.
Let the fire of the Holy Ghost consume those arrows right now in
Jesus' name!
In the name of Jesus, I raise a standard
Against the handwriting of ordinances written against my life.
Let the fire of the Holy Ghost consume any satanic ordnance
Published against me, right now in the name of Jesus.
In the name of Jesus, I issue a decree and a signpost against you, Satan.
In the name of Jesus, there shall be no stopping in my
environment.
In the name of Jesus there shall be no packing in my territory.
In the name of Jesus there shall be no standing by my home.

In the name of Jesus, I command you to keeping moving to the Dead Sea
And remain there in the Dead Sea until your judgment day.

Declaration of Solution
In the name of Jesus,
And with the authority in the blood of Jesus,
I declare the Word of the Lord
Against the arrows that flies by day
And the terror that comes by night.
Psalm 91:1–9 declares,
"He that dwelleth in the secret place of the most High
Shall abide under the shadow of the Almighty.
I will say of the Lord,
He is my refuge and my fortress: my God; in him will I trust.
Surely he shall deliver thee from the snare of the fowler,
and from the noisome pestilence.
He shall cover thee with his feathers,
and under his wings shalt thou trust:
his truth shall be thy shield and buckler.
Thou shalt not be afraid for the terror by night;
nor for the arrow that flieth by day;
Nor for the pestilence that walketh in darkness;
nor for the destruction that wasteth at noonday.
A thousand shall fall at thy side,
and ten thousand at thy right hand;
but it shall not come nigh thee.
Only with thine eyes shalt thou behold
and see the reward of the wicked.
Because thou hast made the Lord,
which is my refuge, even the most High, thy habitation."
Therefore, I declare and decree the word of the Lord upon my life,
That the Lord is my refuge and my habitation.
With the authority in the blood, I declare and decree that the
arms of sorrow and death
Shall not strike my blessings—in Jesus' name.

With the authority in the blood, I declare and decree that the
arrows of death
Shall not frustrate my blessings—in Jesus' name.
With the authority in the blood, I declare and decree that the
arrows of financial debt and poverty
Shall not strike my wealth and prosperity—in Jesus' name.
With the authority in the blood, I declare and decree that the
arrows of divorce and separation
Shall not strike my marriage—in Jesus' name.
With the authority in the blood, I declare and decree that the
arrows of witches and wizards
Shall not strike my family—in Jesus' name.
With the authority in the blood, I declare and decree that the
arrows of anger and strife
Shall not strike my relationships—in Jesus' name.
With the authority in the blood, I declare and decree that the
arrows of hatred and bitterness
Shall not strike my relationships cycle—in Jesus' name.
With the authority in the blood, I declare and decree that the
arrows of envy and jealousy
Shall not strike or disrupt my progress—in Jesus' name.
With the authority in the blood, I uproot any satanic arrow
Sent against me—in Jesus' name.
I declare and decree, let the fire of the Holy Ghost destroy the
Arrows that fly by day and the terror by night.
I declare and decree, let the blood of Jesus nullify every demonic
arrow planted
Against my life and destiny—in Jesus' name.
I declare and decree, let the fire of the Holy Ghost consume the
arrows of destruction and death
That are thrown toward my life and destiny—in Jesus' name.
I declare and decree, let the blood of Jesus build a wall of
protection around me—in Jesus' name.
I declare and decree, let the fire of the Holy Ghost build a hedge
of fire around my life and destiny—in Jesus' name.
Hallelujah, I am free in the name of Jesus. Amen!

Motivational Song of Victory

"And Can It Be That I Should Gain?"
Words: Charles Wesley, *Psalms and Hymns,* 1738
Music: "Sagina," Thomas Campbell, *Bouquet,* 1825

> And can it be that I should gain
> An interest in the Savior's blood?
> Died He for me, who caused His pain—
> For me, who Him to death pursued?
> Amazing love! How can it be,
> That Thou, my God, shouldst die for me?
> Amazing love! How can it be,
> That Thou, my God, shouldst die for me?
>
> 'Tis mystery all: th'Immortal dies:
> Who can explore His strange design?
> In vain the firstborn seraph tries
> To sound the depths of love divine.
> 'Tis mercy all! Let earth adore,
> Let angel minds inquire no more.
> 'Tis mercy all! Let earth adore;
> Let angel minds inquire no more.
>
> He left His Father's throne above
> So free, so infinite His grace—
> Emptied Himself of all but love,
> And bled for Adam's helpless race:

'Tis mercy all, immense and free,
For O my God, it found out me!
'Tis mercy all, immense and free,
For O my God, it found out me!

Long my imprisoned spirit lay,
Fast bound in sin and nature's night;
Thine eye diffused a quickening ray—
I woke, the dungeon flamed with light;
My chains fell off, my heart was free,
I rose, went forth, and followed Thee.
My chains fell off, my heart was free,
I rose, went forth, and followed Thee.

Still the small inward voice I hear,
That whispers all my sins forgiven;
Still the atoning blood is near,
That quenched the wrath of hostile Heaven.
I feel the life His wounds impart;
I feel the Savior in my heart.
I feel the life His wounds impart;
I feel the Savior in my heart.

No condemnation now I dread;
Jesus, and all in Him, is mine;
Alive in Him, my living Head,
And clothed in righteousness divine,
Bold I approach th'eternal throne,
And claim the crown, through Christ my own.
Bold I approach th'eternal throne,
And claim the crown, through Christ my own.

Prayer Observations and Experiences

Write down your observations and experiences as you say this prayer.

You may remember your dreams and some past occurrences while you are saying it. You may also receive a revelation. It is important that you make notes for future reference.

Observations

_____

_____

_____

_____

_____

Experiences

_____

_____

_____

_____

_____

Chapter Twenty-Two

Spiritual Missiles

Spiritual missiles are sudden attacks that are aimed at causing destruction without prior warning. They are spiritual raids that the enemy carries out against a person. They are a form of satanic terrorism.

A spiritual missile is a spiritual bombing that is targeted against a person, an entity, or a place. It is a deliberate accident caused by satanic agents and demonic activities.

A spiritual missile is an act of voodoo and witchcraft. It is the kind of charm, amulet, or gunshot that the enemy releases against an individual or a family. Spiritual missiles are also generated out of envy and jealousy against a person's success and prosperity. Psalm 18 describes them as the arrows of death.

In an academic environment, students who indulge in diabolical activities or demonic spiritism use spiritual missles to charm successful students. Sometimes, demonic charms are rubbed on students' beds, reading tables, chairs, pens, and books or study materials.

For instance, whenever a spiritual missile is sent against brilliant or successful students, such victimized students are demoralized or paralyzed at the edge of celebration or the peak of achievement. Sometimes, a few days before graduation, one of the most brilliant or distinguished students will suddenly fall ill and die. Other times, some few weeks before final examinations, a student will end up in the hospital or have an accident.

Sometimes, parents who are jealous of other children's destinies may influence their wards to carry out demonic terrorism in classrooms and on campuses. Similarly, some students are involved in secret cults in which satanic activities are carried out to stall fellow students' success and destroy the lives of those whom they envy or hate. In recent times, malicious activities have become common among students who want to attain great height in the secular realm without investing much effort in their academic endeavors.

Also in the secular sector, many working-class people are seeking promotion by indulging in diabolical activities as they consult witchdoctors and spiritualists for charms and amulets to wield their power against colleagues on the job. Usually, the individuals involved in demonic aspirations are vicious in their behavior and attitude. They act very suspiciously and often raise false accusations against innocent individuals who are targeted for dismissal, demotion, unemployment, poverty, and lifetime depression.

Attack from spiritual missiles may cause any of the following:
- Sudden death
- Sudden termination of lives involving a whole family
- Undetermined ghastly accidents
- Sudden destruction of a business
- Sudden imprisonment
- Sudden termination of employment
- Sudden financial mishap
- Sudden ailment or incurable disease
- Sudden interference with success and promotion
- Sudden halt in wealth and prosperity

More often than not, workers of iniquity release agents of curses and spiritual missiles in the form of worms, rodents, and pests against other people's business ventures, such as manufacturing industries, agricultural farms, plantations, retail stores, distribution outlets, restaurants, or food-packaging industries.

It is imperative that we commit everything we do to God in prayer so that all our plans can materialize just as we hope they will. This is because the enemy likes to attack or frustrate our plans and steer us away from our destiny.

Spiritual Missiles Launched at Destiny Fulfillment: The following testimony is an example of how the plans of man can be foiled and frustrated and all his hopes dashed within a short space of time. Names have been changed to protect the individuals' privacy.

Spikey and Caddy's Story

Spikey and Caddy were two students who were classmates in the same university. They were both from very poor financial backgrounds. They were also the first to attend college in their families and were therefore the pride and joy of their parents and extended families. Spikey was on full scholarship, and that was a big relief to his family since they did not have to worry about the financial aspect of seeing their son through university.

Caddy, on the other hand, was not fortunate enough to get a full scholarship. As a matter of fact, he did not get any scholarship at all. He had to depend on student loans to see him through college. Even getting those loans was not easy; it was difficult for him to get a cosigner, as he did not have any form of credit. His parents also had bad credit as a result of all the financial problems they had. Therefore they could not cosign for him. A friend of the family who saw all of Caddy's potential decided to help him out and cosign for him to get the loan that would enable him to go to the university and make his family proud.

However, it was still not easy for him and his family since the loan was not enough to afford him a comfortable living situation on campus. His parents had to provide him with some money from time to time for his upkeep, and that took a big toll on their finances. They still tried their best, hoping that Caddy would get a good job when he graduated and all their financial problems would be solved.

Caddy and Spikey became friends on campus and were almost inseparable. They believed they had a lot in common as a result of their backgrounds. They studied together and did almost everything together. They seemed to have a bond that could not be easily broken. In fact, people thought they were siblings.

Toward the end of their second year, Spikey suddenly became very ill. He couldn't keep anything down and was losing a lot of weight. He was admitted to the hospital, where a lot of tests were performed in an attempt to find what was ailing him, but to no avail. He slipped into a coma about two weeks after being admitted to the hospital, and died five days later. Spikey's parents and his entire family were heartbroken. They mourned the loss of their son and also the death of their dreams. All their aspirations were crushed. It felt like their world had come to an end. Their most intelligent son, who had a lot of potential to make it in life, had suddenly been stolen away by death. A son who was supposed to be the hope of their lives had been taken from their midst by the arrows of death.

Hence, Caddy was also heartbroken. He had lost his best friend and study partner. He was devastated and felt very lonely without his friend. He tried to fill the void in his life by concentrating on his studies and studying more than ever. This resulted in his grades getting better than they had been, and that made his parents more proud of him. They couldn't help but brag to their friends about how intelligent their son was. They talked about him to everyone who would listen.

Caddy made it to his final year in college and was looking forward to graduating. He had high hopes for his future and already knew which organization he wanted to work with and had started making contacts there. His networking seemed to be paying off since the company was also eager to have him work with them. However, about two weeks before his final exams, he suddenly fell ill just like his friend Spikey, and died. This was a devastating blow to the family. His parents were crushed as their hopes and plans for their son were crushed. He had not been able to live long enough to graduate from the university and relieve them of their financial burdens. There was also their son's student loan to be paid off, which they just couldn't afford. The cosigner of Caddy's loan was also putting pressure on them to pay off the loan, because he did not want to end up having to pay for it himself.

Some of the students started talking about how the death of the two friends could not be coincidental. They believed there was something more to it than met the eye. The parents of both boys also believed the death of their sons could be a result of envy and jealousy from some members of their families or workers of iniquity in their environments.

The powers of warfare prayers could have intercepted the missiles that were being thrown toward those who perished. That is why it is important to be very prayerful and commit all our endeavors into the hands of God.

Everyone is vulnerable as we live with and dwell among people with different belief systems from diverse backgrounds. Some people are good and others are evil. Some people believe in helping others succeed and rise up to their oriented destiny, whereas others believe in stealing, killing, or destroying other people's successful destiny. No matter what the matter may be or the situation is, a relationship with the Lord is the key to long life, good health, and prosperous destiny. Let's learn to pray to God and war against our common enemy.

Note Page

_____

_____

_____

_____

_____

_____

_____

_____

_____

_____

_____

_____

_____

_____

_____

Strategic Solution Prayer Against Satanic Terrorism and Spiritual Missiles

The Problem
There are constant attacks on my life that affect my spouse, children, business, and everything else.

The Situation
I have frequent mishaps and accidents.
Suddenly I have financial distress.
Suddenly I have business interruptions and transaction failures.
There are untimely ailments and deaths at the points of achievement.
There are frequent fatal interruptions at the time of celebration and ovation.
I am experiencing constant harassment from demonic entities.

The Goals
I need to uproot the curses of enchantment and divination.
I will destroy the signs of divination.
I will destroy the signposts of satanic habitation from my dwelling places.
I will combat the attacks of satanic worms that eat from my blessings.
I will exterminate the worms that bite into my progressive fruitfulness.
I will establish a signpost of no entry against satanic invasion into my territory.
I will build a stronghold against satanic harassment.

Authority of Scripture
Joel 1:1–7

The word of the Lord that came to Joel the son of Pethuel. Hear this, ye old men, and give ear, all ye inhabitants of the land. Hath this been in your days, or even in the days of your fathers? Tell ye your children of it, and let your children tell their children, and their children another generation. *That which the palmerworm hath left hath the locust eaten; and that which the locust hath left hath the cankerworm eaten; and that which the cankerworm hath left hath the caterpiller eaten.* Awake, ye drunkards, and weep; and howl, all ye drinkers of wine, because of the new wine; for it is cut off from your mouth. For a nation is come up upon my land, strong, and without number, whose teeth are the teeth of a lion, and he hath the cheek teeth of a great lion. He hath laid my vine waste, and barked my fig tree: he hath made it clean bare, and cast it away; the branches thereof are made white. (Emphasis added.)

Prayer in Action
(Praise, Worship, and Adoration)
Jehovah God, the King of Glory,
You are worthy to be praised and exalted.
You are worthy of all adoration.
There is none like you and none to be compared.
You are the great "I Am."
You are the Alpha and Omega, the beginning and the end.
You are the God of wars, the one who fights victoriously.
You are the God who delivers and sets free from evil.
Great are You, Lord. Great is the work of Thy hands.
Hallelujah! To God be the glory; great things He has done.
Amen!

Environmental Protection
In the name of Jesus,
And with the authority of the blood
That was shed on the cross of Calvary,
Let my life be protected from satanic missiles.

Let my soul be saturated with the blood of Jesus against
diabolical activities.
Let my life be surrounded by the fire of the Holy Ghost
That consumes evil missiles.
Let my family and household be hidden under the shadow
Of the Almighty.
Let the blood of Jesus raise a wall of defense over our destiny
Against all manner of evil intentions and spiritual missiles.
In the name of Jesus Christ, my Lord and Savior, I pray. Amen!

Warfare and Confrontation
In the name of Jesus,
And with the authority of the blood
That was shed on the cross of Calvary,
I raise a standard against satanic missiles
That confront me in the daytime and by night,
In the spiritual and physical realms,
And in every realm of my existence.
In the name of Jesus, I come against the weapons of spiritual missiles
That are sent against me,
To cause mishaps and accidents in my environment
And to steal away the lives of family members.
In the name of Jesus, I release the blood of Jesus
Against the yoke of financial debt, accidents, sickness, terminal
diseases, employment depression, promotional suppression,
academic oppression, and social frustration.
In the name of Jesus Christ, my Redeemer,
I uproot and cast out the weapons of destruction
Mounted against my wealth and prosperity.
In the name of Jesus Christ, my Savior,
I uproot and cast out all manner of satanic assaults and violations
That are listed against me and my family's destinies.
In the name of Jesus, I uproot the trees of satanic missiles
Planted or buried with my name and image
From the graveyard of destruction.
In the name of Jesus, I uproot and cast out
The elements of curses buried against my elevation.
In the name of Jesus, I release myself from weapons of envy and jealousy

Mounted against my destiny.
In the name of Jesus, I command the fire of the Holy Ghost to destroy
The root of all manner of spiritual missiles in my life.
In the name of Jesus, let brimstone fire from above
Consume the root and manifestation of spiritual missiles
That interfere with my life and destiny.
In the name of Jesus,
I release my life and my name, my home and my family,
My job and my finances, and all that belongs to me
From diabolical activities, satanic assaults, and violations,
And I declare my environment out of bounds to the enemy.
I command a total eviction and destruction of handwritings of ordinances
That permit the enemy to have access against my life.
In the name of Jesus, I command a seal against every door
That permits the enemy to gain access to my life.
In the name of Jesus, I declare and decree no entry into my life.
In the name of Jesus, the enemy shall no longer gain access
To assault and violate my life and that of my family.
In the name of Jesus, today shall be the last time
The enemy will terrorize my life with satanic missiles
To cause havoc and destruction in my destiny. Amen!

Declaration of Solution
In the name of Jesus,
And with the authority in the blood of Jesus,
I stand on the authority of the Word of God
To declare a war against demonic divination conjured against me.
In the name of Jesus, I uproot and cast out the
Spirit of divination sent against me in the
Spiritual and natural realm, the material financial realm,
And also in the emotional and marital realm.
In the name of Jesus, I declare that any form of divination conjured
shall not influence or cause me to suffer any kind of accident.
Therefore, you, spirit of accident, shall not drive with me—in Jesus' name.
With the authority of the blood, you, demon of accident, shall not
sit with me—in Jesus' name.

With the authority of the blood, you, demon of accident, shall not wait for me on the road—in Jesus' name.
With the authority of the blood, you, demon of accident, shall not control my mind—in Jesus' name.
The blood of Jesus raises a standard against you.
Get out of my body, soul, and spirit—in Jesus' name.
In the name of Jesus, I declare and decree that the demons of divination shall not control or manipulate my daily endeavors.
In the name of Jesus, I declare and decree that the demons of confusion Shall not control or manipulate my marriage.
I declare and decree, let the blood of Jesus nullify your activities.
I declare and decree, let the fire of the Holy Ghost consume your works.
I declare and decree that Satan and his cohorts shall no longer see me or come to visit me—in Jesus' name.
I declare and decree that demons shall no longer harass or terrorize my destiny—in Jesus' name.
I declare and decree that whatever I have bound on earth is bound in heaven,
And whatever I have loosed on earth is loosed in heaven—in Jesus' name. Amen!

Motivational Song of Victory

"Love Divine, All Loves Excelling"
Words: Charles Wesley, 1747
Music: "Beecher," John Zundel, *Christian Heart Songs,* 1870

Love divine, all loves excelling,
Joy of heaven to earth come down;
Fix in us thy humble dwelling;
All thy faithful mercies crown!
Jesus, Thou art all compassion,
Pure unbounded love Thou art;
Visit us with Thy salvation;
Enter every trembling heart.

Breathe, O breathe Thy loving Spirit,
Into every troubled breast!
Let us all in Thee inherit;
Let us find that second rest.
Take away our bent to sinning;
Alpha and Omega be;
End of faith, as its Beginning,
Set our hearts at liberty.

Come, Almighty to deliver,
Let us all Thy life receive;
Suddenly return and never,
Never more Thy temples leave.

Thee we would be always blessing,
Serve Thee as Thy hosts above,
Pray and praise Thee without ceasing,
Glory in Thy perfect love.

Finish, then, Thy new creation;
Pure and spotless let us be.
Let us see Thy great salvation
Perfectly restored in Thee;
Changed from glory into glory,
Till in heaven we take our place,
Till we cast our crowns before Thee,
Lost in wonder, love, and praise.

Prayer Observations and Experiences

Write down your observations and experiences as you say this prayer.

You may remember your dreams and some past occurrences while you are saying it. You may also receive a revelation. It is important that you make notes for future reference.

Observations

_____

_____

_____

_____

_____

Experiences

_____

_____

_____

_____

_____

Part 8

Realms of Fulfillment

Chapter Twenty-Three

Inheritance

A inheritance is a legacy that one is entitled to, by virtue of belonging and having a legal relationship with someone. Usually, a person is entitled to a possession by birthright. For instance, children are naturally entitled to their parent's properties. Also, siblings are naturally expected to inherit from one another, especially if some of them have no spouse or children.

Similarly, spouses are natural beneficiaries of each other's inheritance with or without children. Generally, family members are a person's heritage.

Act of Appreciation: In some cases, people or organizations that have provided some form of help or assistance to support a person's progress or advancement in life may also benefit from an individual's legacy.

Act of the Devourer: Sometimes, individuals who have been appointed as executors or given power of attorney have held on to the properties concerned and never released it to the individuals to whom the inheritance was bequeathed.

There are destiny switchers and twisters who waggle their way through clairvoyance and diabolical devices in order to take over or succeed certain inheritances that belong to other people. Sometimes, sudden association with deceitful individuals or the appearance of demonic strangers has robbed some individuals of their birthright. For instance, workers of iniquity may use charms, witchcraft spells, or divination and some form of diabolism to mesmerize individuals to sign over their inheritance to them, in the absence of family members.

Whatever the situation may be, you can work out a procedure to claim your inheritance. The following prayers will help you regain what you have lost.

Claiming My Possession and Inheritance

Exodus 9:29
And Moses said unto him, As soon as I am gone out of the city, I will spread abroad my hands unto the Lord; and the thunder shall cease, neither shall there be any more hail; that thou mayest know how that the earth is the Lord's.

Deuteronomy 10:14
Behold, the heaven and the heaven of heavens is the Lord's thy God, the earth also, with all that therein is.

Psalm 24:1–5
A Psalm of David. The earth is the Lord's, and the fullness thereof; the world, and they that dwell therein. For he hath founded it upon the seas, and established it upon the floods. Who shall ascend into the hill of the Lord? or who shall stand in his holy place? He that hath clean hands, and a pure heart; who hath not lifted up his soul unto vanity, nor sworn deceitfully. He shall receive the blessing from the Lord, and righteousness from the God of his salvation.

Note Page

Strategic Solution Prayer to Possess My Inheritance

The Problem
I need full access to my inheritance.

The Situation
Strangers have taken over my legal possession.
Executors are holding on to my properties.
Executors have refused to put my name on legal documents.

The Goals
The executors will release my properties to me.
Those strangers will no longer hold on to my blessings.
Those workers of iniquity will not have access to my possessions.
There shall be no envy and strife over my inheritance.
The Lord will fight every battle that concerns my inheritance.
The Lord will dismantle the conspiracy of robbery intended
against my possessions.
No one will switch or twist my inheritance.
There shall be no enchantment against me because of my blessings.

Authority of Scripture
Genesis 30:25–33; Joshua 14:11–13 and 15:19–20

Genesis 30:25–33,
And it came to pass, when Rachel had born Joseph, that Jacob said
unto Laban, Send me away, that I may go unto mine own place,
and to my country.
Give me my wives and my children, for whom I have served thee,
and let me go: for thou knowest my service which I have done thee.
And Laban said unto him, I pray thee, if I have found favour in
thine eyes, tarry: for I have learned by experience that the Lord
hath blessed me for thy sake.
And he said, Appoint me thy wages, and I will give it.
And he said unto him, Thou knowest how I have served thee, and
how thy cattle was with me.
For it was little which thou hadst before I came, and it is now
increased unto a multitude; and the Lord hath blessed thee since my
coming: and now when shall I provide for mine own house also?
And he said, What shall I give thee? And Jacob said, Thou shalt
not give me any thing: if thou wilt do this thing for me, I will
again feed and keep thy flock:
I will pass through all thy flock to day, removing from thence all
the speckled and spotted cattle, and all the brown cattle among
the sheep, and the spotted and speckled among the goats: and of
such shall be my hire.
So shall my righteousness answer for me in time to come, when
it shall come for my hire before thy face: every one that is not
speckled and spotted among the goats, and brown among the
sheep, that shall be counted stolen with me.

Joshua 14:11–13,
As yet I am as strong this day as I was in the day that Moses sent
me: as my strength was then, even so is my strength now, for war,
both to go out, and to come in.
Now therefore give me this mountain, whereof the Lord spake
in that day; for thou heardest in that day how the Anakims were
there, and that the cities were great and fenced: if so be the Lord
will be with me, then I shall be able to drive them out, as the Lord said.

And Joshua blessed him, and gave unto Caleb the son of
Jephunneh Hebron for an inheritance.

Joshua 15:19–20
Who answered, Give me a blessing; for thou hast given me a south
land; give me also springs of water. And he gave her the upper
springs, and the nether springs.
This is the inheritance of the tribe of the children of Judah
according to their families.

Prayer in Action
(Praise, Worship, and Adoration)
Praise God from whom all blessings flow.
Praise Him all creatures here below.
Praise Jehovah God, the King of Glory.
Praise the Creator of the universe.
Praise the Maker of mankind.
He is the Alpha and Omega.
He is the all-knowing God.
Excellent is His name forever. Amen!

Environmental Protection
In the name of Jesus,
And with the authority of the blood
That was shed on the cross of Calvary,
Let my life be protected from *destiny switchers and twisters.*
Let my soul be saturated with the blood of Jesus against diabolical
activities.
Let my life be surrounded by the fire of the Holy Ghost
To consume the activities of conspiracy meant against me.
Let my properties and inheritance be hidden under the shadow
Of the Almighty.
Let the blood of Jesus raise a wall of defense over my destiny
Against all manner of evil intentions and divinations.
In the name of Jesus Christ, my Lord and Savior, I pray. Amen!

Warfare and Confrontation
In the name of Jesus,
And with the authority of the blood
That was shed on the cross of Calvary,
I raise a standard against satanic intentions
That confront me by day and by night,
In the spiritual and physical realms
And in every realm of my existence.
In the name of Jesus, I come against the weapons of deception
That are mounted against my prosperity
To cause poverty and lack in my environment,
And to steal away the inheritance that belongs to me.
In the name of Jesus, I release the blood of Jesus
Against the thieves and robbers of my destiny
Who have refused to release my possession to me.
In the name of Jesus, I command the body, soul, and spirit of the
executors of my properties to release them to me right now.
In the name of Jesus, let the executors of my properties not have
peace or rest until they have turned over my inheritance.
In the name of Jesus, there shall be no frustration and oppression
of my life
In the matter of releasing my property.
In the name of Jesus Christ, my Redeemer,
I uproot and cast out the weapons of destruction
Mounted against my wealth and prosperity.
In the name of Jesus Christ, my Savior,
I uproot and cast out all manner of satanic assaults and violations
That are listed against me and my family's destinies.
In the name of Jesus I uproot the trees of clairvoyance and
divination
Planted or buried against my name and image
In the graveyard of destruction.
In the name of Jesus I uproot and cast out
The elements of curses buried against my prosperity
from the crown of my head through to the soul of my feet.
In the name of Jesus I release myself from weapons of envy and jealousy
Mounted against my destiny.

In the name of Jesus, I command the fire of the Holy Ghost to destroy
The root of all manner of divination planted against my life.
In the name of Jesus, let brimstone fire from above
Consume the root and manifestation of deception and divination
That interferes with the possession of my inheritance.
In the name of Jesus,
I release my life and my name,
My home and my family, my inheritance,
My job and my finances, and all that belongs to me
From the diabolical activities, satanic assaults, and violations,
And I declare my environment out of bounds to the enemy.
I command a total eviction and destruction of handwritings of ordinances
That permit the enemy to have access to my properties.
In the name of Jesus, I command a seal against every door
That permits the enemy to gain access to my possessions.
In the name of Jesus I declare and decree no entry into my life.
In the name of Jesus, the enemy shall no longer gain access
To assault and violate my life.
In the name of Jesus, today is the last time.
The enemy will no longer terrorize my life
To cause havoc in my destiny. Amen!

Declaration of Solution
In the name of Jesus,
And with the authority in the blood of Jesus,
I clear up my land and possession from any satanic inhabitants.
No powers or principalities of darkness
And rulers or satanic hosts shall inhabit my inheritance—in Jesus' name.
The word of God declares in Deuteronomy 10:14,
"Behold, the heaven and the heaven of heavens is the Lord's thy God,
the earth also, with all that therein is."
Psalm 24:1–5 also says,
"A Psalm of David.
The earth is the Lord's, and the fullness thereof;
the world, and they that dwell therein.
For he hath founded it upon the seas,
and established it upon the floods.
Who shall ascend into the hill of the Lord?

or who shall stand in his holy place?
He that hath clean hands, and a pure heart;
who hath not lifted up his soul unto vanity, nor sworn deceitfully.
He shall receive the blessing from the Lord,
and righteousness from the God of his salvation."
Therefore, Satan, listen to me,
You and your cohorts shall not interfere
With my possession and inheritance—in Jesus' name.
With the authority in the name of Lord, I release the blood of Jesus
To build a covering over my spiritual and physical properties,
Material and financial possessions, emotional and marital land.
According to the Word of the Lord,
"The earth is the Lord's and the fullness thereof."
It is also written and commanded in Genesis 1:28,
"Subdue the earth and have dominion over it."
Therefore I possess my land of inheritance—in Jesus' name.
I clear up my land from any demonic habitation—in Jesus' name.
I declare and decree that no rogue shall inhabit my land of inheritance.
The spirit of the dead shall not reside on my inheritance.
In the name of Jesus, I evict and evacuate
Ghost and haunting demons out of my land.
I evict you, demon spirit, and evacuate you out of my possession.
In the name of Jesus, go out of properties and possessions.
In the name of Jesus, go out of habitations and environments.
In the name of Jesus, go out of life and families.
The blood of Jesus repels you from my possessions.
The fire of the Holy Ghost consumes you and your activities—in
Jesus' name.
I declare my land and possessions free from satanic harassment—
in Jesus' name.
I invite the presence of the Lord to take over my possessions and
inheritance.
I declare that the Lord shall be the host over my possessions and
inheritance.
I declare the blood of Jesus as my insurance against evil.
I declare the blood of Jesus as my protection and security against demons.
Thank You, Lord, for providing security and assurance
Over my inheritance. Amen!

Motivational Song of Victory

"No, Not One!"
Words: Johnson Oatman Jr., 1895
Music: George C. Hugg

There's not a friend like the lowly Jesus,
No, not one! No, not one!
None else could heal all our soul's diseases,
No, not one! No, not one!

Refrain

Jesus knows all about our struggles,
He will guide till the day is done;
There's not a friend like the lowly Jesus,
No, not one! No, not one!
No friend like Him is so high and holy,
No, not one! No, not one!
And yet no friend is so meek and lowly,
No, not one! No, not one!

Refrain

There's not an hour that He is not near us,
No, not one! No, not one!
No night so dark but His love can cheer us,
No, not one! No, not one!

Refrain

Did ever saint find this Friend forsake him?
No, not one! No, not one!
Or sinner find that He would not take him?
No, not one! No, not one!

Refrain

Was ever a gift like the Savior given?
No, not one! No, not one!
Will He refuse us a home in Heaven?
No, not one! No, not one!

Prayer Observations and Experiences

Write down your observations and experiences as you say this prayer.

You may remember your dreams and some past occurrences while you are saying it. You may also receive a revelation. It is important that you make notes for future reference.

Observations

_____

_____

_____

_____

_____

Experiences

_____

_____

_____

_____

_____

Chapter Twenty-Four

Fulfillment

Destiny Fulfillment

Fulfillment comes after one has gone through the process of planting and harvesting one's effort with satisfaction. Where there is no sowing, there is also no reaping. One can harvest only what one has planted. The process of destiny is a progressive system of making conscious and unconscious efforts toward achievements and fulfillments. Life is progressive only when one is actively involved in each destination that is connected to one's destiny.

As the overall discussion of this book comes to a conclusion in this chapter, it is pertinent to examine the act of progressiveness as an element of solution in connection to fruitfulness and fulfillment. Fulfillment is something that one has to learn to achieve during one's prime age and not at the end of life. Fulfillment of people's efforts should be connected to their destiny, so that they can relate their achievement to the hope and aspirations in which they invested from early childhood. A lifetime of aspirations are often connected to one's destiny. Destiny is satisfied whenever a plan and purpose is accomplished. Therefore,

- destiny should be fulfilled when one is actively involved with life.
- destiny should be fulfilled when one is youthful and useful.
- destiny should be fulfilled when one has the ability to celebrate one's effort with others.
- destiny should be fulfilled when one can encourage others to carry on with one's achievement.
- destiny should be fulfilled when one can use one's experience to mentor others.
- destiny should be fulfilled when one can gracefully reproduce one's success to the benefit of younger generations.
- destiny should be fulfilled when one is able to share one's experience with others.

Planting System

Planting is a process of sowing a specific type of seed, with an expectation of reaping a certain type of fruit. There are different types of sowing in the natural and spiritual realm that affect human endeavors.

Natural and Physical Planting

A person's life is like a garden, a farmland, a field, an orchard, or a plantation. The type of seed that one carries determines what kind of planting one does. A perishable vegetable seed cannot be sown in a plantation. Rice seeds cannot be sown in a garden.

A person's ability determines what kind of planting he or she can afford.

Spiritual Planting

Spiritual planting is a type of farming that requires natural consciousness. Without a physical effort, spiritual planting cannot take place. For instance, in the spiritual realm, speaking or talking is a type of sowing seed. Speaking is a natural effort that produces spiritual omen. A conscious effort is needed to activate things from the spirit realm into reality. Thus, an effort is needed to *call forth that which is not as though they were*. Until there is a speaking, there is no planting. Until there is an active effort, there is no sowing of seed.

Before anything happens in the natural realm, it has already taken place in the spiritual realm. That is why we usually dream about an event before it is manifested in the physical realm. Dreams are supposed to be revelations of events that take place in the realms of the spirit that are intended for natural activities. Not all dreams are revelations, because a person's thoughts can influence a dream.

Therefore, in order to penetrate the realm of the spiritual, you must indulge in praying out your desire and expectation. Prayer is communication with the realms of the spirit. In the act of prayer, one is either communicating with the Almighty God or with the god of this world (Satan and his powers and principalities of darkness). Prayer is also a confrontation or war against the enemy, whereby you speak directly or indirect against the enemy and his operations.

Spiritual planting declares and decrees the Word of the Lord into the garden of one's life to establish a purpose on earth as it in heaven. To indulge in the act of spiritual planting, one needs to be connected to the Almighty God through a relationship with Christ Jesus, our Lord and Savior, as discussed in the foundational relationships in the early chapters of this book. (See my book *Strategic Prayer Tactics* for details.)

Giving as Planting

Also, the work of one's hand, in the realms of giving, is a process of planting what one expects to receive. Any time a person gives freely to another person or organization, one is sowing a seed that will generate increase in multiples.

Therefore, plant your seed for goodness in a fertile ground and you will reap in abundance.

- Plant your seed with generosity.
- Plant your seed with genuineness.

Process of Solution

More often than not, solution springs out of words spoken to provide instruction and direction to people from childhood to adulthood. Parents start a process of raising a child by teaching and instructing from day one till the age of accountability. Solution is an active process that requires individuals' attention and involvement.

Prayer requires an individual's effort and indulgence. An individual's contribution to one's endeavor paves the way for progress to take place. "From whom the whole body fitly joined together and compacted by that which every joint supplieth, *according to the effectual working in the measure of every part, maketh increase of the body* unto the edifying of itself in love" (Ephesians 4:16). (Emphasis added.)

Whenever an individual makes a conscious effort toward an action or a program, that effort results in a kind of achievement that may be favorable or unfavorable. An unfavorable result is not the end of the program but an opportunity to explore new methods toward a better outcome. Where an effort yields a good result, there is room for advancement. Therefore, as one continues to invest more effort into a program or project that is bearing fruits, one's effort becomes progressive. And of course, progressive effort that is fruitful brings satisfaction and fulfillment.

Hence, scripture says, "The effectual fervent prayer of a righteous man availeth much" (James 5:16).

The words of our mouths are seeds that are sown when we make utterances: "That the communication of thy faith may become effectual by the acknowledging of every good thing which is in you in Christ Jesus" (Philemon 1:6).

- A positive utterance germinates a good tree and bears a good fruit.
- A positive word spoken is sharing a good plant with another person.
- A positive language spoken is spreading one's plantation around for the benefit of others.
- Plant good seed into other people's lives and expect the same.

- Plant your blessings and expect a great harvest of honor and respect.
- Plant your seed and expect abundance.

Harvesting and Fulfillment

Solutions to problems are a type of harvest after an effort. Harvest is a product of a progressive effort that one invests in one's endeavor. An act of seeking, searching, knocking through persistent prayer, and fasting would yield harvest of fruitfulness that satisfies one's soul and destiny.

If you have read and prayed using the variety of prayers presented in this book, you can expect to have an abundance of harvest that will satisfy your expectations.

- Harvest time is a season of fruitfulness.
- Harvest time is a season of accountability.
- Harvest time is a season of enjoyment.
- Harvest time is a season of satisfaction.
- Harvest time is a season of celebration.
- Harvest time is a season of achievement.
- Harvest time is a season of fulfillment.
- Harvest time is a season of blessing.

Isaiah 5:1–2
Now will I sing to my wellbeloved a song of my beloved touching his vineyard. My wellbeloved hath a vineyard in a very fruitful hill: And he fenced it, and gathered out the stones thereof, and planted it with the choicest vine, and built a tower in the midst of it, and also made a winepress therein: and he looked that it should bring forth grapes, *and it brought forth wild grapes.* (Emphasis added.)

Matthew 13:24
Another parable put he forth unto them, saying, The kingdom of heaven is likened unto a man which sowed good seed in his field: But while men slept, his enemy came and sowed tares among the wheat, and went his way. But when the blade was sprung up, and

brought forth fruit, *then appeared the tares also.* So the servants of the householder came and said unto him, Sir, didst not thou sow good seed in thy field? from whence then hath it tares? He said unto them, *An enemy hath done this.* The servants said unto him, Wilt thou then that we go and gather them up? But he said, Nay; lest while ye gather up the tares, ye root up also the wheat with them. (Emphasis added.)

Note Page

Strategic Solution Prayer
to
Plant My Life and Endeavors on Fertile Grounds

The Problem
I will recognize my seeds and season for sowing.

The Situation
I will understand the realms of planting.
I will identify the kind of soil that I possess in the realms of the spirit.
I will determine the kind of seeds that should be sown during a specific season.
I will recognize and stay connected to the Lord of my harvest.
I will spread my seeds around to assist others.

The Goals
I will be fruitful in life and in all my endeavors.
I will be planted by living waters for abundance.
I will be fruitful in season and out of season.
I will stay connected to the Lord of my harvest.
I will not sow tares in my vineyard.
I will be wise and skillful in all realms of my existence.
My life will be progressive and fulfilling.

Authority of Scripture
Psalm 1:1–6 and 92:5–14

Psalm 1:1-6

Blessed is the man that walketh not in the counsel of the ungodly, nor standeth in the way of sinners, nor sitteth in the seat of the scornful.
But his delight is in the law of the Lord; and in his law doth he meditate day and night.
And he shall be like a tree planted by the rivers of water, that bringeth forth his fruit in his season; his leaf also shall not wither; and whatsoever he doeth shall prosper.
The ungodly are not so: but are like the chaff which the wind driveth away.
Therefore the ungodly shall not stand in the judgment, nor sinners in the congregation of the righteous.
For the Lord knoweth the way of the righteous: but the way of the ungodly shall perish.

Psalm 92:5-14

O Lord, how great are thy works! and thy thoughts are very deep.
A brutish man knoweth not; neither doth a fool understand this.
When the wicked spring as the grass, and when all the workers of iniquity do flourish; it is that they shall be destroyed for ever:
But thou, Lord, art most high for evermore.
For, lo, thine enemies, O Lord, for, lo, thine enemies shall perish; all the workers of iniquity shall be scattered.
But my horn shalt thou exalt like the horn of an unicorn: I shall be anointed with fresh oil.
Mine eye also shall see my desire on mine enemies, and mine ears shall hear my desire of the wicked that rise up against me.
The righteous shall flourish like the palm tree: he shall grow like a cedar in Lebanon.
Those that be planted in the house of the Lord shall flourish in the courts of our God.
They shall still bring forth fruit in old age; they shall be fat and flourishing;

Prayer in Action
(Praise, Worship, and Adoration)
O Lord, my God,
You are awesome.
You are worthy to be praised.
You are worthy to be adored.
You are worthy to be exalted far above the heavens.
Great and mighty are the works of Your hands.
There is none like You.
No one else can touch my heart like You do.
Excellent is Thy name.

Environmental Protection
In the name of Jesus,
And with the authority of the blood
That was shed on the cross of Calvary,
Let my life be protected from satanic utterances.
Let my soul be saturated with the blood of Jesus against negative
pronouncements.
Let my life be surrounded by the fire of the Holy Ghost
That consumes evil missiles.
Let my family and household be hidden under the shadow
Of the Almighty.
Let the blood of Jesus raise a wall of defense over the destiny of my family
Against all manner of evil utterances and pronouncements.
In the name of Jesus Christ, my Lord and Savior, I pray. Amen!

Warfare and Confrontation
In the name of Jesus,
And with the authority of the blood
That was shed on the cross of Calvary
I raise a standard against satanic trees planted
To confront me by daytime and by night
In the spiritual and physical realms,
And in every realm of my existence.
In the name of Jesus, I come against the weapons of satanic verses
Written and spoken against me,
To cause suppression and frustration in my environment,

And to steal away the joy of my strength.
In the name of Jesus, I release the blood of Jesus
Against the yoke of demonic seeds that produce
Evil thorns and thistles in my vineyards.
In the name of Jesus Christ, my Redeemer,
I uproot and cast out the weapons of destruction
Mounted against my wealth and prosperity.
In the name of Jesus Christ, my Savior,
I uproot and cast out all manner of satanic verses
That are written against me and my family's destinies.
In the name of Jesus I uproot the trees of demonic pronouncements
Planted or buried against my name and image in the graveyard
of destruction.
In the name of Jesus I uproot and cast out the elements of curses buried
Against my elevation from the crown of my head down to the
soles of my feet.
In the name of Jesus, I release myself from weapons of envy and jealousy
Mounted against my destiny.
In the name of Jesus, I command the fire of the Holy Ghost to destroy
The root of all manner of spiritual missiles in my life.
In the name of Jesus, let brimstone fire from above
Consume the root and manifestation of contamination and pollution
That interfere with my life and destiny.
In the name of Jesus, I release my life and my name,
my home and my family, my job and my finances, and all that
belong to me
From diabolical activities, satanic assaults, and violations,
And I declare my environment out of bounds to the enemy.
I command a total eviction and destruction of handwritings of ordinances
That permit the enemy to have access against my life.
In the name of Jesus, I command a seal against every door
That permits the enemy to gain access to my life.
In the name of Jesus, I declare and decree no entry into my life.
In the name of Jesus, the enemy shall no longer have access
To hinder progressiveness in my endeavor.
In the name of Jesus, today shall be the last time
The enemy will terrorize my life with stagnancy and retrogression
To cause delay or denial in my destiny. Amen!

Declaration of Solution

In the name of Jesus,
And with the authority in the blood of Jesus,
I declare that evil seeds
Shall not be planted on my land of possession.
In the name of Jesus, I uproot and cast into fire
Any seed of corruption and contamination
That was planted day or night.
I release the fire of the Holy Ghost to consume
The tare and thistles planted to destroy my harvest.
The blood of Jesus exterminates any demonic weeds
Planted in my vineyard of prosperity.
In the name of Jesus, I sow the seeds of my blessings onto my vineyard.
In the name of Jesus, I declare and decree that my land shall be fertile.
In the name of Jesus, I declare and decree that my land shall flow
with milk and honey.
In the name of Jesus, I declare and decree that there shall be no
drought or famine on my land.
In the name of Jesus, I declare and decree that the land of my
heart shall flourish in righteousness.
In the name of Jesus, I declare and decree that I shall bear fruit of
righteousness.
In the name of Jesus, I declare and decree that the land of my
womb shall be fertile.
And I shall be fruitful and multiply—in Jesus' name.
In the name of Jesus, I declare and decree that the land of my tongue
shall prosper
And the words of my mouth shall be fruitful.
In the name of Jesus, I declare and decree that the steps of my feet
shall be ordered by the Lord,
And I shall be instructed and directed into my destiny.
In Jesus' name I pray. Amen!

Song of Motivation

"Praise God, from Whom All Blessings Flow"
(Doxology)
Words: Thomas Ken, 1674. These lyrics, sung as the Doxology
in many churches, are actually the last verse of a longer hymn,
"Awake, My Soul, and with the Sun."
Music: "Old 100th," *Genevan Psalter*, 1551, attributed to Louis
Bourgeois

> Praise God, from Whom all blessings flow;
> Praise Him, all creatures here below;
> Praise Him above, ye heavenly host;
> Praise Father, Son, and Holy Ghost.

Prayer Observations and Experiences

Write down your observations and experiences as you say this prayer.

You may remember your dreams and some past occurrences while you are saying it. You may also receive a revelation. It is important that you make notes for future reference.

Observations

_____

_____

_____

_____

_____

Experiences

_____

_____

_____

_____

_____

Reflection

The purpose of this book is to enable people to make amendments wherever they have made some mistakes that have caused them to slump into a state of stagnancy, retrogression, and depression. For a person to gain full recovery and start off in a progressive pathway, it is important to reflect on the notes that one has jotted down on each chapter of this book. It is also important to do some specific reflections, because a general reflection may be productive but not effective. Reflection is a process of examining the lessons that you learned from reading or studying this book. For instance, it is wise to answer the questions below in order to experience the effectiveness of this book, as you may be expecting a real makeover in your life.

What have you learned?

_____

_____

_____

_____

How will you apply the lesson learned to your life?

_____

_____

_____

_____

How will you use the lesson learned to assist others?

_____

_____

_____

_____

What are the challenges or hindrances you are encountering?

_____

_____

_____

_____

Find out if God has ever spoken to you. What did God say, and what did you hear?

_____

_____

_____

_____

Are you in the right profession? Are you in the right place?

_____

_____

_____

_____

What is progress? And what is fruitfulness to you? Can you identify your progressiveness and fruitfulness?

_____

_____

_____

_____

What is your level of fulfillment?

_____

_____

_____

_____

What have you discovered about yourself?

_____

_____

_____

_____

What are the specific instructions and strategies that you want to adopt in order to live a progressive life?

_____

_____

_____

_____

Asking for a progressive fruitfulness means you want the will of God to be done on earth as it is in heaven. Do really want His perfect or permissive will?

_____

_____

_____

_____

What are the areas in which you need fruitfulness?

_____

_____

_____

_____

Identify your challenges.

_____

_____

_____

_____

Identify your weak points and shortcomings.

_____

_____

_____

_____

Do you have a teachable spirit?

_____

_____

_____

_____

How often have you changed relationship because of hurt or anger?

_____

_____

_____

_____

Whenever you come across stagnancy in the course of an aspiration, do you withdraw from the duty? What do you do to effect corrections in order not to fail again?

_____

_____

_____

_____

How do you react when someone points out your errors or weaknesses?

_____

_____

_____

_____

Do you get angry, or do you work toward change?

_____

_____

_____

_____

Prayer Observations and Experiences

Write down your observations and experiences as you say this prayer.

You may remember your dreams and some past occurrences while you are saying it. You may also receive a revelation. It is important that you make notes for future reference.

Observations

_____

_____

_____

_____

_____

Experiences

_____

_____

_____

_____

_____

Bibliography

1. *Matthew Henry's Commentary on the Whole Bible.* Peabody, Mass.: Hendrickson Publishers, 1992.
2. *Thompson Chain Reference Study Bible,* New King James Version. Indianapolis: Thomas Nelson, 1997.
3. *Oxford Dictionary and Thesaurus.* New York: Oxford University Press, 1996.
4. Walley, Pauline. *Strategic Prayer Tactics I: Effective Communications with Aromatic Expressions.* New York: Xulon Press, 2006.
5. Walley, Pauline. *Strategic Prayer Tactics II: Effective Deliverance Prayer Tactics—Warfare and Confrontations.* New York: Xulon Press, 2006.
6. Walley, Pauline. *Strategic Prayer Tactics I: Effective Prayer Communications with Aromatic Expressions.* New York: Xulon Press, 2007.
7. www.answers.yahoo.com.
8. www.cyberhymnal.org.
9. www.e-sword.software.informer.com.
10. www.freechristianresources.org/2007-06/esword-review.
11. www.hymnsite.com.
12. www.wikipedia.org.
13. www.hymnlyrics.org.

Appendixes

Decision

If you have never surrendered your life to Jesus Christ as your Lord and Savior, then it is important for you to do so right away. Otherwise it will be difficult for you to conquer anger and overcome the negatives ruling your life. If you are willing to accept Jesus Christ as your Lord and Savior, then pray like this:

> *Lord Jesus, I come to You just as I am. Forgive me my sins and deliver me from all works of iniquity.*
>
> *Deliver me from all the evil characteristics and behaviors that have kept me in bondage.*
>
> *Set my soul and spirit free to worship You in spirit and in truth.*
>
> *Come into my life and make me whole.*
>
> *I need You, Lord. I need You every hour unto eternity. Amen.*

Rededication

If you have never made a decision to surrender your life to Jesus Christ and you have been struggling with the Christian life, or you are somehow an active Christian but are still struggling with some ungodly characteristics and behaviors, then you need to rededicate yourself to the lordship of your Jesus. Make a total surrender so that the enemy will not have any form of control at all in your life. You may pray like this:

Lord Jesus, teach me to surrender my total being to Your Lordship and control so that the enemy will no longer have a part in me. Teach me to abide in You so that You will also abide in me and dwell in my life.

Teach me to study Your Word and make a conscious effort to apply it to my daily living.

Wash me, cleanse me, and purify my spirit, soul, and body so that I may be acceptable in Your sight.

Thank You, Lord, for delivering me from the works of iniquity. Amen.

Pauline Walley Deliverance Bible Institute & Prophetic-Deliverance Training and Theological Institute
(School of Intensive Training for Ministry and Leadership Equipment)

The Pauline Walley Deliverance Bible Institute is a school of intensive training that equips and trains leaders, individuals, and church groups in the ministry. It is an intensive, practical training center where people are taught to build their images and personalities, improve their ministry skills and abilities, develop their talents and gifts, and minister to themselves, family members, friends, churches, and/or fellowship members. In the process of training, people are also taught for ministration and facing the battle of life as it is in the ministry.

The areas of study include the following:
- School of Deliverance
- School of Strategic Prayer
- School of Tactical Evangelism
- School of Mentoring and Leadership
- School of the Gifts of the Holy Spirit

- School of the Prophets
- School of Prophetic Deliverance
- School of Prophetic Intercession
- School of Ministerial Responsibilities and Church Administration

The Pauline Walley School of Intensive Trainings are held in different parts of the world at various times. At the seminar levels, one week or two weeks of intensive training help leaders and ministers or church/fellowship groups establish various arms of church ministry and equip their members for such purposes.

Biweekly intensive training programs, the one-year certificate course, and degree programs are readily available in the Bronx, New York, and other regions based on request. If you are interested in hosting any of these programs in your region, country, or church/ministry, please contact us. See details about our contact information and website on the back page.

Christian Books by
Dr. Pauline Walley

The Authority of an Overcomer: You Can Have It ... I Have It
  The Authority of an Overcomer shares the real-life testimony of a day-to-day experience with the Lord Jesus Christ. It encourages you to apply the Word of God to every facet of your life, such as sleeping and waking with Jesus, walking and talking with Jesus, and dining with Him as you would with your spouse or a friend.

Somebody Cares ... Cares for You ... Cares for Me
  Somebody Cares ... Cares for You ... Cares for Me talks about the care that the Lord Almighty has for every one of us. It teaches you to care for other people and exercise tolerance toward their shortcomings. You will learn the importance and the true meaning of love as you read this book.

Receive and Maintain Your Deliverance on Legal Grounds
  Many people go from one prayer house to another, from the general practitioner to the specialist, from one minister to the pope, and from one chapel to another church with the same mission and

the same expectation, yet never hit the target. Why? Many people lack the knowledge of how to maintain their healing and deliverance. This book, *Receive and Maintain Your Deliverance on Legal Grounds*, will teach you how to maintain what you receive from God.

Anger: Get Rid of It ... You Can Overcome It
Anger is one of the many problems that many seek to resolve but for which they lack the solution. Many have resigned their fate to it, thinking that it is a natural phenomenon. *Anger: Get Rid of It ... You Can Overcome It* teaches about the causes of anger and how to uproot them to receive your healing.

The Power of the Spoken Word
There is a purpose for which we speak, and when we speak, we expect something to happen so the purpose of the utterance will be fulfilled. *The Power of the Spoken Word* teaches you to exercise your authority so that the words you speak will be manifested effectively.

The Holy Spirit: The Uniqueness of His Presence
The presence of the Holy Spirit highlights the differences between the gifts of the spirit, the presence of God, and the visitation of the Holy Spirit. In *The Holy Spirit: The Uniqueness of His Presence,* you will learn to enjoy the delightful presence of the Holy Spirit in your spiritual walk.

The Holy Spirit: Maintain His Presence in Trials and Temptations
The Holy Spirit: Maintain His Presence in Trials and Temptations teaches you how to maintain the presence of God, especially during trials and temptations. Oftentimes when Christians go through difficult situations, they think they are alone, but they need not feel that way. You can enter the presence of the Holy Spirit in difficult times and witness His power to strengthen you and turn your situations around.

The Holy Spirit: Power of the Tongue

In recent times, many people have been seeking instant power and prophetic manifestations. Christians and ministers are indulging in all sorts of practices to demonstrate some special abilities to attract public attention. This book, *The Holy Spirit: Power of the Tongue*, discusses the various powers and anointing(s) at work. It will help you decipher between the Holy Spirit's power and satanic powers. It will also teach you about the various anointing(s) that exist and how you can reach out for the genuine one.

Pulling Down Satanic Strongholds: War Against Evil Spirits

Many Christians are under satanic attacks and influences, but very few people understand what the actual problems are. Some believe in God but have no idea that there is anything like the satanic realm; however, they are under satanic torments. This book, *Pulling Down Satanic Strongholds*, enlightens you on some of the operations of the devil. It will help you know when an activity being performed around you is of the devil. This knowledge will strengthen you in prayer and equip you against the wiles of the enemy.

When Satan Went to Church

Many people fear the devil more than they fear God. At the mention of Satan or demons, they are threatened to death. Yet they are complacent in their own ways and yield to sin easily. Let the fear of God grip you, and not the fear of Satan. *When Satan Went to Church* enlightens you about the activities of the enemy within and around the church, the home, and the Christian community. It helps you identify battles and put on your armor of warfare against the enemy. It also encourages you to hold firmly the shield of faith. May the Lord enlighten your eyes of understanding as you read this book.

Solution: Deliverance Ministration to Self and Others

Since the death of Jesus Christ on the cross, humans have been given the opportunity to experience and encounter the joy of salvation. However, lack of knowledge has kept the world in the dark and deprived it of the importance of Christianity. This book, *Solution: Deliverance Ministration to Self and Others,* portrays just what the title says. It teaches you to understand the intricacies of deliverance ministration and to avoid the dangerous practices that have discouraged others. Read it, and you will be blessed as never before.

Strategic Prayer Tactics I: Effective Communications with Aromatic Expressions

This book, *Strategic Prayer Tactics I,* with its focus on the types and approaches to prayer, teaches you how to approach the throne of God with a specific need and the strategies to adopt for its presentation. It also teaches you to pray with scripture as your legal authority. Read it, and you will be blessed as never before.

Strategic Prayer Tactics II: Effective Deliverance Prayer Tactics. Warfare, and Confrontations. Approach to Effective Communication in Prayer.

This book, *Effective Deliverance Prayer Tactics II,* teaches you how to separate your personal identity from demonic apparitions that emanate from ancestral curses. It also teaches you how to pull down satanic strongholds that interfere with your family by using scripture as your legal authority. Read it, and you will be blessed as never before.

School of Mentoring and Leadership I: The Act of Mentoring

- Stirring Up, Activating, and Imparting
- Talents and Abilities for Effectiveness

We all have talents and abilities that need to be developed in order for us to achieve our ambitions. Many people are bedeviled by unfulfilled dreams and are wallowing in familiar oppression and depression. *School of Mentoring and Leadership I* will help you locate and choose a mentor who will help you discover and develop your abilities and lead you to the fulfillment of your ambition. This course will teach and draw you closer to your destiny. Stay blessed and enjoy the act of mentoring.

School of Mentoring and Leadership II: Progressive Achievement—Receive It, Maintain It. The Act of Self-Mentoring

This book, *Progressive Achievement: Receive It, Maintain It,* teaches you how to mentor yourself while you move in progression to overcome obstacles that would usually frustrate prosperity. It enlightens you about the various types of progress that may come your way and how to manage it. It also encourages you to overcome failure and disappointment. The book helps you to understand the concept of self-mentoring in the course of progressiveness as part of the characteristics of the Holy Spirit.

School of Prophetic Deliverance: Understand the Language, Interpretations, and Assignments

Everyone believes that he or she is a child of God. Unfortunately, not everyone hears the voice of the Father, and not all are close to Him; however, all are seeking His divine attention. *School of Prophetic Deliverance I* will teach the basic principles of the prophetic ministry and also give you the basic understanding of the prophetic word and its operations. The understanding of the prophetic word will draw you closer to Him as never before. Stay blessed and enjoy the prophetic realm.

Destiny Solution Prayers: Lord, Make Me Over

Destiny Solution Prayers: Lord, Make Me Over is about how to get a hold of destiny. It discusses the various activities that connect one destination with ano ther on the pathway to destiny. It teaches you how to recognize and respond to the voice of destiny. Each chapter provides you with a notepad for reflection, a prayer, and a motivational song that will encourage you to make over your life in order to fulfill your destiny with satisfaction. This book is a trip that guides you to walk the path of destiny with understanding and wisdom.

Subscription

Gospel Songs on Cassette
- "Overcomers' Expression"
- "Send Your Power"
- "Vessels of Worship"
- "Poetic Expression"

BOOKS
All the books listed are available in bookstores and by order.

UNITED KINGDOM
Pauline Walley Christian Communications
P.O. Box 977, Aylesbury, Buckinghamshire, HP20 9HD
Tel: (+44) 7960-838-012

UNITED STATES
Pauline Walley Christian Communications
P.O. Box 250, Bronx, NY 10467
Tel: (718) 652-2916
Fax: (718) 405-2035
E-mail: admin@paulinewalley.org
Web site: www.school-of-deliverance.com
www.paulinewalley.org
www.paulinewalley.com
www.pwdi.org

ABOUT THE BOOK

The word *progress* brings to mind promotion, advancement, wealth, and prosperity, and the term *fruitfulness* causes one to visualize the variety of juicy fruits, such as ripened mangoes, oranges, passion fruits, nectarines, bananas, and so on. As the title goes, so is the content.

Progressive Solution Prayers: Fruitfulness and Fulfillment is a prayer book that discusses the common problems that people face in everyday life and provides strategic solutions with the aid of scripture-based intercessory and warfare prayers that teach you how to approach the throne of God in a focused and strategic manner. The book shows you how to apply different types of prayers to specific issues relating to you and your loved ones in order to achieve results.

The prayer topics range from situations concerning your progressiveness in the natural, spiritual, and secular realms to the realm of relationships. The book also teaches you how to pray effectively to uproot curses and every evil seed that has been planted in your land of possession.

Furthermore, it provides you with the wisdom to break through any evil that holds you in some sort of bondage. It teaches you to offer effective prayers that transform problems into lifetime solutions.

Read these prayers aloud to yourself and meditate on the scriptures from which they are based and your life will never be the same. Stay blessed!

ABOUT THE AUTHOR

Pauline Walley-Daniels, PhD, is an ordained prophetic-deliverance apostle who teaches the word of God with dramatic demonstrations. She is the president of Pauline Walley Evangelistic Ministries and Christian Communications and the CEO of the Pauline Walley Deliverance Bible Institute as well as the Prophetic-Deliverance Training and Theological Institute, which includes the School of Intensive Training for Leadership and the School of Deliverance in New York.

Dr. Pauline is affiliated with the Christian International Ministries Network, International Coalition of Apostles, and is the vice president of Fellowship of Ministers International. She serves on the Christian Life Educators Network board of regency.

She holds a master's degree in journalism and a doctorate in pulpit communications and expository preaching. Dr. Pauline is the author of twenty books and is married to Rev. Frederick Daniels of Overcomers' House Prophetic-Deliverance Church in the Bronx, New York.